W9-CGR-282

THE POINT AFTER

THE
POINT AFTER

SEAN CONLEY

LYONS
PRESS

Guilford, Connecticut

An imprint of The Rowman & Littlefield Publishing Group, Inc.
4501 Forbes Blvd., Ste. 200
Lanham, MD 20706
www.rowman.com

Distributed by NATIONAL BOOK NETWORK

British Library Cataloguing in Publication Information available

Library of Congress Cataloging-in-Publication Data available

ISBN 978-1-4930-4276-0 (cloth : alk. paper)
ISBN 978-1-4930-4277-7 (electronic)

♾™ The paper used in this publication meets the minimum requirements of American National Standard for Information Sciences—Permanence of Paper for Printed Library Materials, ANSI/NISO Z39.48-1992.

CONTENTS

PREGAME

kick·er

noun

1. a person or animal that kicks.
2. an unexpected and often unpleasant discovery or turn of events.

It's the biggest night of my life, October 10, 1992. Tonight Pitt will play the most storied team in college football, the University of Notre Dame. The Fighting Irish had 11 National Championships, seven Heisman Trophy winners, and their own television contract with NBC. Games can be lost or won by a point. My job is to make extra points and field goals. I'm the kicker.

I rush into the trainers' room to be sure I get my favorite trainer, Rick. Seven long tables are already occupied with players receiving their last-minute treatments, massages, oral painkillers. Players getting their ankles taped stare at the ribbons of tape circling their ankles. Taping's an art. It has to be done just right. My guy, Rick, waits by the empty table with one hand on his hip and the other holding a heating device.

I take my shirt off and climb up on my belly, bracing myself for electrical stimulation. Rick unscrews the cap of something that looks like a giant tube of toothpaste. He squirts some gel on white pads and places them on my lower back. After countless sessions, the gooey sensation still makes me squirm. Rick sticks two white electrode squares on each side of my spine right above my tailbone. "Are they in the right spot?" he asks.

"Perfect." As usual. Somehow he remembers every inch of every player's injury.

Barely audible hip-hop thumps from the locker room on the other side of the blue door. The cross-chatter in the trainers' room drowns it out. "We got over 40 guys that need treatment before the game tonight,"

Rick tells me. It's been two months since the first day of training camp and injuries are piling up.

He turns the dial in slow motion.

"Enough?" he asks.

My lower back feels like hundreds of ants are biting it.

"A little more."

I want it to work. I *need* it to work.

"Did you take your muscle relaxant yet?" Rick asks me.

"Just half. The whole pill makes me drowsy."

While the timer is on, I try to relax and picture myself kicking the ball. The self-talk began the night before in my hotel bed and will not subside. *I can't miss any kicks tonight. Don't choke.* I imagine being successful and picture myself kicking the ball through the uprights. My battle with confidence and fear goes back and forth. Confidence wins. I haven't missed a field goal in a month. I'm in the zone. I'm more excited than nervous.

Being a kicker is a lonely job. In the NFL, each team carries just one. One kicker. No backup. You're it. I can be a hero or the goat of the game. To keep from going crazy, I talk to myself. Like I'm living on a deserted island. And very often, the self-talk makes me crazy. My opponents are the wind, the cold, and the 10-foot-high and 18½-foot-wide crossbar, and 30-foot-high metal posts that I have to kick the ball through, but also anxiety, fear, and worry. My allies are confidence and hitting the ball just right. Not too hard, not too soft, and in the right spot. The sweet spot. A tiny spot about the size of a nickel near the tip of the ball. Missing it by a sliver can send the ball careening outside the uprights and my mood into the pits of despair.

I remind myself to think positive. I picture my kicks flying through the middle of the uprights. I recollect specific kicks I've made in the past. Rutgers—dead center from 44 yards. Minnesota—from the left hash, 42 yards.

I tell myself to relax. Don't change anything. Nice and easy.

As a kicker, there's not much upside. You're expected to make every kick.

There's no coasting when you're a kicker, no resting on your laurels. It's always, *What if I miss the next kick? Then what?*

Just one kick can change a kicker's career. Make one and you ride a wave of confidence for days. Miss one and you may fall into depression. The feeling of letting your whole team down can make you a head case. How a kicker responds to adversity can shape his entire career. You have to be resilient and bounce back after a miss.

The kick is either good or no good. There are no points for how far it goes or if it hits the upright. It's hard not to translate this into *I'm* either good or no good.

As I relax on the table, almost to the point of napping, a gorgeous brunette with an infectious smile pops in my mind. I hope she will be watching the game tonight. And then, the stim machine beeps and jolts me back to reality.

Rob, our head trainer, stops by my table and says, "You're going to have a great game tonight. I can feel it." He is one part athletic trainer, one part Zen master.

I make a quick visit to see the ball boy. I can't control the wind tonight, but I can control the balls I'll kick. I examine the balls marked with a black K. I squeeze them and rub my hands all over them. With both hands, I press the ends in to soften the points. Every little detail counts. They feel perfect.

I tell him, I like these two best.

He will make sure the refs use them for my field goals.

At my locker, I stretch my black nylon ankle brace over my left foot. I sprained my ankle in high school playing basketball and it has never been the same since. I pull my socks up right beneath my calf muscles, then put my Nike turf shoe on my left foot and tug the laces as tight as possible. I'm on my second pair of laces this season due to pulling them too hard. I pop my right foot into my Adidas soccer shoe. I filed down the cleats on the bottom to reduce friction on the artificial turf. Everything needs to be perfect.

I stretch my blue and yellow jersey with the large #2 over my shoulder pads, then contort and slither my chest and arms to get all the way in. I stare for a moment at my helmet hanging on the inside of my locker and feel adrenaline surging inside my veins. I grab it by the facemask and head toward the tunnel to go onto the field for pregame warmups. I feel like I have to go to the bathroom. It's the nerves.

When I return to the locker room, the stereo is off.

"Get yourselves ready, guys," the linebacker coach says.

I pull my Discman out of my backpack and cue up my traditional pregame warmup song: Guns N' Roses, "Welcome to the Jungle." About a hundred other guys look just like me, quiet and expressionless. The room is focused, on edge. Once the song ends, I toss my Discman back in the bag and begin my personal meditation. I visualize myself making the big kick. Everyone else is imagining similar success stories. Our star quarterback, Alex Van Pelt, is making the big pass. Dietrich Jells, our standout wide receiver, is grabbing the pivotal catch.

I have dreamed of a day like today since the day I finished in third place at the Punt, Pass, and Kick competition that my dad took me to when I was eight. A little kid with a bowl cut, a smile, and freckles, I'd told my dad, "I'm going to play in the NFL someday." I'll never know if he believed me, but he never pushed me. But he didn't have to. Growing up, I kicked for hours at a nearby dirt field in my hometown of Erie, Pennsylvania, until the sun went down. It felt more like play than practice.

Football was everything to me. I watched it every weekend with my dad: college football on Saturdays, the NFL on Sundays. I wanted so badly to be on a team, to be part of something bigger than myself. I wanted to win the ultimate team championship, the Super Bowl. Fourteen years later and 120 miles from home, I'm closer to that dream coming true than almost any one of the millions of kids who'd fantasized about it.

The guy next to me says, "There are scouts from every NFL team here tonight. I saw ones from the Detroit Lions and the Dallas Cowboys."

"Are you shitting me?" someone says.

I scan the room and catch nervous glances.

Each one of us knows that to win, we need every yard, every inch. Scrape and claw. Play above ourselves. We are a struggling team. Three losses already. We can erase all the disappointment with a win tonight. The entire country is watching.

A calm voice interrupts the tension. "Gentlemen, bring it in."

Paul Hackett, our head coach, wears a crisp white oxford shirt and blue-striped tie, and as he walks, he puts his Pitt hat on over his curly hair, giving it a small adjustment. We gather in the center of the room and take a knee on the floor, keeping a little opening for Coach Hackett to get into the center of our circle. In the distance, we hear a buzz. We are in the belly of the old concrete Pitt Stadium. There are 52,000 people in the stands. We can't see the fans yet, but we can feel them.

"Gentlemen, this is why you came to Pitt." He looks us in our eyes, one by one. "To play on the biggest stage in college football."

The head referee comes in and interrupts the moment: "Coach, we need your captains on the field now." I grab my helmet and walk over to him at the locker room exit. Cornerback Vernon Lewis, #42, the captain of the defense, joins us. And then Alex Van Pelt, our quarterback, #10, the captain for the offense. I'm the captain of the special teams.

The referee takes a look at his oversized wristwatch. "Let's go, guys," he says, and walks down the tunnel. I've walked through this cold tunnel dozens of times, but tonight it feels warm from the excitement in the air. We grab each other's hands and walk out side by side. As we start down the tunnel, we can hear cleats on the cement, but as we approach the field, the vibration from the drums of the Pitt band and the cheers from the crowd swallow us, and my blood is flowing full throttle.

We slow our pace for a moment to take it in. We emerge into the hazy October night. As I step out of the tunnel, I feel like a gladiator walking into the Coliseum. The sky is shades of orange and purple. The stadium lights are on full blast. Over my left shoulder, the Pitt student section waves their yellow pompoms in unison with the band. The air is buzzing. Over my right shoulder, in the corner of the end zone, it's a sea of green. It's the Notre Dame section. Their mascot, a leprechaun, dances for the crowd.

Men in red ESPN jackets walk around with cameras on their shoulders. A couple dozen photographers with zoom lenses larger than their arms congregate by the goalposts behind the end zone.

I wonder what my parents are thinking right now. They traveled two and a half hours. They are now somewhere in the sea of blue and yellow. When I was a kid, my dad would call me into the TV room on crisp

Saturday afternoons. "Notre Dame is on." This was the equivalent of his saying, "It's time for church."

My father didn't attend Notre Dame or live near South Bend, Indiana. I once asked him, "Why do we root for Notre Dame?"

"Because we are Irish *and* Catholic."

When I kicked those field goals until the sun set behind the trees, I imagined I was playing for Notre Dame.

The rest of the referees stand at midfield. Approaching from the far right sideline are two extraordinary Notre Dame players: #6, Jerome Bettis, nicknamed "The Bus" because of his ability to carry would-be tacklers on his back as if they were passengers along for a ride, then #3, quarterback Rick Mirer. Both were preseason candidates for the Heisman Trophy, the award given to the most outstanding player in college football, and potential NFL first-round draft choices. I glance over to the sideline and see legendary coach Lou Holtz in his blue windbreaker, pacing like a nervous squirrel before the game has even begun. He had led Notre Dame to become national champions just three years earlier.

The Notre Dame players come charging out of the tunnel on the northern end of the stadium. Their seating section erupts in euphoria as the rest of the stadium boos. The boos shift again to cheers as the rest of our team comes rushing out of the opposite end. The stadium is now in controlled chaos.

"Shake hands, gentlemen," the head referee says.

I stand across from Bettis, surprised that I'm taller. But his extra 50 pounds of muscle still manage to make me feel small. He sways back and forth with a grin like a boxer getting ready for a title match. Rick Mirer is cool and calm. At 6'3", he has the preppy looks of a fraternity brother.

My back feels good. Adrenaline and drugs are masking the pain.

My butterflies are gone. I'm laser focused.

Our team comes out strong. About five minutes in, I line up for a 20-yard field goal. Kickers don't believe in the term "chip shot." Each kick packs pressure. They are expected to make almost every kick, especially the short ones. I don't change my mechanics. I use the same leg swing. I make the field goal for a 3–0 Pitt lead. I breathe out. The kick boosts my confidence and builds rhythm.

After the Irish respond with a touchdown to make it 7–3, we head toward another score. As our offense crosses the 50 yard line, I begin warming up on the sideline. It's been almost a month since I've missed a field goal, but I'm starting to feel the pressure. The face of the girl that I'm hoping to impress enters my mind, and I wonder if she is watching right now in a crowded bar. I offered her a ticket, but she was stuck waitressing. We have been dating for just a month, and this would be her first time seeing me play.

Our drive stalls on their 31 yard line after an incomplete pass. It will be a 48-yard field goal attempt. "Field goal team!" shouts Amos Jones, the special teams coach.

We line up on the field. I take my customary three steps back and one and a half steps over. Every seat in the stadium is filled, but I can't hear the crowd over the beating of my own heart. I glance at the Notre Dame players getting ready to try to block my kick and time stops. It's just me, the green turf, and my holder and snapper.

My holder, J. R., is on his knee ready to receive the snap. He looks back at me to see if I am ready. I nod. The ball zips into his hands. A second later, I strike it clean. I complete my follow-through, look into the illuminated sky, and see the ball floating high through the air end over end toward the white goalposts.

CHAPTER 1
KICKOFF

Sunlight shimmered on the snow outside. It looked like another foot had fallen overnight. Through a murmur of voices outside, I could hear shovels scrape as they found pavement beneath on the sidewalk.

Erie was in the midst of a brutal winter in 1978, and that morning was the first in weeks that I had seen the sun. It seemed like it had snowed every day. In Erie, it was either winter, almost winter, or just after winter.

The smell of bacon found its way up to the second floor. I slid down the stairs and skidded into the kitchen where my mom was fixing scrambled eggs, bacon, sausage, and orange juice. The front page of the *Erie Daily Times* showed a picture of dozens of men ice fishing on Lake Erie and a story about someone walking the 24 miles from Erie over the frozen lake to Canada. Mom told me to get bundled up and sent me outside to help my dad shovel. On my way out the door, I grabbed my football.

My father was a security guard for the Lord Corporation on 12th Street, a wide road of bustling manufacturing plants. He had a second job installing alarms for ADT. From time to time, he would get laid off from his job at Lord. When that happened, he would work at my school, Sacred Heart, as a janitor. I would tag along and he would assign me to sweep the gym floor and underneath the wooden bleachers.

He was a local sports legend, a fixture on the sandlots. In his younger years, he'd been Pennsylvania All-State in football, baseball, and basketball. He was 5'10", brawny and strong, with dirty blond hair and a bald spot halo on top. His blue eyes expressed warmth and humor, and even in his late 40s, he could swing a baseball bat as smoothly as Hank Aaron.

The youngest of five kids, his dad died when he was 15, so when he was offered a minor-league contract with the Pittsburgh Pirates, he instead chose the Army to help pay the family bills.

That spring, I joined a soccer team, and I was the worst kid on the team. The coach played me the least and put me where I'd encounter the minimum amount of action. The next season, I practiced hard and scored 18 goals. I wanted to be a great athlete just like my dad. I figured that what I lacked in raw talent I could make up for in sheer desire and work ethic.

One weekend on our way back from my dad's softball game when I was eight years old, we stopped into the Chestnut Street Pub for a beer, a pop, and sour cream and onion potato chips. Bars and churches were easy to find in Erie. While other patrons played pinball, drank drafts, and watched baseball on television, we talked about kicking and soccer. "What do you think about signing up for Punt, Pass, and Kick?"

"What's that?"

My dad explained that it was a football competition in which the kids got one chance to punt, one to pass, and one to kick. The judges would add up all the distances, and the ones who scored the highest won. The top three kids got a trophy.

"Sure, dad," I said. "I'll do it."

So, on a brisk fall morning, after my two bowls of Cap'n Crunch cereal, I laced up my cleats, grabbed my tee and my football, and jumped into the front seat of our Impala station wagon. No seatbelt needed in 1978.

Waterford, Pennsylvania, was a sleepy little town, home to the historic Eagle Hotel, a stone building like hundreds of old inns on the Eastern Seaboard, proclaiming that "George Washington slept here." Misty rain left the field of the high school where we'd be competing soggy and smelling like manure. I looked around at the other 50-some kids. They looked big enough to have mustaches.

"How old are these kids?"

"Well, the competition is for 8-, 9-, and 10-year-olds. I'm guessing most of them are 10."

I felt like peeing my pants.

We started with the pass, which meant throwing the ball as far down the field as possible. When my turn came up, I heaved it as far as I could, and it sailed a nice distance. Next came the punt, which meant dropping the ball onto the top of your foot and kicking it as far and as straight as possible. I dropped the ball onto my foot, and it flew off my foot like a rocket, sailing past all the markings.

My dad was keeping tabs from the sidelines. "You're in first place by a mile. You just need a decent kick and you'll be the winner," he said.

When the time came to kick, I placed the ball on the tee with my hands trembling, then walked back five yards. I gazed at the ball, approached with a slow jog, and then struck it as hard as I could. It whimpered less than 10 yards from the tee and ended a slow death rolling along the wet grass. I blew it. I went from first to third.

My dad just shrugged and said, "Let's go get a pop."

My disappointment lasted just seconds. I didn't care that I hadn't finished first, or that I had botched the kick. And neither did my dad. I was eight and it was fun. That's the same outlook I would need years later. But I was hooked. That night, I began sleeping with my football.

• • •

Playing with a football in the grass made me feel alive. In the classroom, I felt trapped. Restless. In class, I'd look out the window and feel like I was going to explode if I couldn't get out of my seat. I would ask the teacher to go to the bathroom and then slip into the gym and grab a basketball until I got sent back by the janitor.

My parents always wondered why I couldn't behave or settle down.

Around the time of my 10th birthday, I went on what I thought was a routine visit to the pediatrician, Dr. Gold. We sat in his waiting room, which featured wall-to-wall wood paneling. My mom wasn't talking as much as usual. Something seemed different. The nurse called us back and led us to a room that looked like a smaller version of the waiting room, with identical paneling and an array of farm-themed pictures including *American Gothic*, with the serious lady and the man holding a pitchfork. If Dr. Gold was trying to scare me before he even entered the room, then mission accomplished.

Dr. Gold looked in my ears and nose and asked me to open my mouth and say *ahh*. Then he looked at my mom.

"How are things?"

"Sean seems to be having some behavior issues," she said.

I wanted to fade into the farm pictures and hide.

She told him about my most recent report card, which had had negative remarks about my conduct, and how the teachers were always complaining about my behavior.

He asked my mom a series of questions, and words came up that I had never heard before: *hyperactive, attention deficit disorder,* and one word over and over: *Ritalin.* Dr. Gold said, "Sean has what we call attention deficit disorder." (Nowadays it's called ADHD, for attention deficit hyperactivity disorder.)

He told us without Ritalin, I'd keep getting in trouble.

Thirty minutes earlier, I'd thought I was normal. Now some doctor was saying I was broken and I needed to be fixed. I didn't want to listen to him.

His sales pitch continued. "This pill will help you calm down and focus. If any kid asks why you're taking it, just tell them you need it to help you concentrate."

I was afraid to respond. I was terrified of him. But in my head, I said no. There was nothing wrong with me. I wasn't sick. He doesn't know me.

Mom wanted the best for me, and she followed the edict that most parents did at the time: *The doctor knows best.* I was a new member of the American Ritalin Explosion Club. In the 1980s, it was estimated that between 200,000 and half a million children were receiving Ritalin. I didn't think I needed to be on any pill, so I decided I wouldn't take it.

That night, my parents argued in the kitchen. My dad, who rarely raised his voice, was angry. He told my mom there was nothing wrong with me. I agreed. I just always wanted to be moving. Playing sports. Daydreaming. Wondering. I didn't see what was wrong with that.

But my mom insisted it was doctor's orders. My mom won.

My mom was the glue that kept our family together. While my father was busy working two jobs, she still managed to work full-time as a middle school teacher, feed me and my siblings, get us where we needed to be, and try to keep me in line. She took pride in her German upbringing and attempted to keep order, religion, and tradition in the home. She was the enforcer.

Each morning, she wrapped my little white "concentration pill" in aluminum foil and put it in my lunch box. The teachers were responsible for observing me as I took my medicine at the lunch table, but they were easy to fool. I pretended to put it in my mouth while chugging it down with a pint of chocolate milk. But secretly, I tucked the white pill in the crust of my Wonder Bread and salami sandwich. I'd eat the whole thing except the last piece where the pill was embedded. Then I tossed it in the garbage.

One day, I got sloppy. Rather than sticking to Operation Wonder Bread, I dropped my medication on the lunchroom floor among the crumbs and wrappers. The tiny pill was somehow discovered by Walter the janitor and traced back to me, The Ritalin Kid.

Now I had to go to the office, where the principal, Sister Mary Joseph, a kind, heavyset woman in her early 70s, watched me put it into my mouth. But even a nun couldn't set me straight. I would spit it out when she turned her back. Then I'd tuck the half-dissolved pill into my pocket. Anything not to take this "you-have-problems" pill. It was like I thought if I wasn't taking the treatment, there was no ailment. The kids in school teased me, calling me "the spaz."

While skipping my pill as often as possible, I started to act out what I thought the medicine was for, figuring if the doctor said I'm hyperactive, then I'll be *more* hyperactive to show them how ineffective their treatment was.

One day in sixth grade, I grabbed a stapler and drove a dozen staples into the seat of the empty desk next to me. The bell rang, and I was off to the next class down the hall. When I came out, standing outside the room with her arms crossed, looking down at me and shaking her head, was Sister Mary Joseph.

I walked into her office, past the wooden Catholic school paddle displayed prominently in the entry. There was a girl in there—crying. She had cut the back of her legs on the staples when she sat down.

The hurt girl looked at me with confusion. Why would I do such a thing? My stomach sank, and I wanted to cry with her.

The incident led to our first family meeting with the principal and the teachers. My mom listened while she sat slouched, bags under her eyes. The conclusion of that meeting was a warning that another "incident" like this could lead to expulsion.

A few weeks later, I was serving mass as an altar boy. It was a funeral mass, so I missed a couple of hours of school. Thinking it would be funny, after mass I went into the closet and stole a bag of hosts, the circular cracker-like bread that the priest places in your mouth as he says, "the body of Christ." It is one of the most sacred acts in the Catholic Church. I brought them to lunch and passed them out like jelly beans to all my friends at the table, saying, "Communion hosts on me!"

But some of the hosts found their way onto the floor. Walter, who must have been the Sherlock Holmes of custodians, found them and notified Sister Mary Joseph.

The meeting was scheduled: me, my parents, my teachers, the principal, and Father David. This had to be it—stealing the body of Christ and passing it out like candy cigarettes. I was a goner.

We sat in the elf-size plastic chairs at a table in the front of the classroom. Seeing a bunch of grownups sit in tiny chairs made me laugh inside, but the amusement was short-lived. I sat up tall and listened when I remembered I might be expelled. My leg shook while they spoke, and I prayed that they wouldn't kick me out. I knew the things I had done were wrong. I just didn't know why I did them.

My teachers and the principal made it clear: They wanted me gone ASAP. But Father David listened quietly with a gentle nod, placing his index finger over his lips and thick red mustache. When it was his turn to speak, I braced myself, ready for him to lower the boom.

"I don't think what Sean did is a big deal," he said. "The hosts weren't even blessed yet."

YES! I thought. *Unblessed hosts. Thank you, Father.*

"If they had been blessed, we'd have a problem. But before communion hosts are blessed, they're just flour, water, yeast, and salt. And besides, he's one of our best altar boys."

The principal's and the teachers' jaws dropped. Father David saved me.

On the drive home, my dad didn't say a word. He stared straight ahead and gripped the steering wheel so hard, I thought he was going to pull it out of the dashboard. I went straight to my room when we got home.

Alone in there, I wondered why I couldn't be a kid who just cooperated and sat at his desk. And was it really a bad thing? Unknown to me at the time, this restlessness was actually a superpower that, when properly channeled, would drive me toward an NFL career with determination and fortitude.

With a second chance, I focused on getting my shit together. Sports made it a whole lot easier. I played all year long, adding basketball and baseball to the roster of activities that would help rein in my energy. I played quarterback, wide receiver, defensive tackle, and kicker for the school's football team. I made it through the next two years with just minor missteps. I promised my mom I would take my Ritalin, but I didn't, and no one knew the difference. When it was all said and done, I had made it through the eighth grade, and all the time I was supposed to be on Ritalin, I probably didn't take more than a dozen of those pills.

I did still struggle to pay attention during school. I had the attention span of a puppy when I was seated in a classroom. It seemed like the only time my mind didn't race was when I was playing sports. Between the Punt, Pass, and Kick contest, my troubles at school, and the relief I felt in being outside and playing sports, it seemed clear. There was one way to succeed and be happy, and that was to play football.

CHAPTER 2
FIRST AND 10

Freshman year. Five seats in front of me sat a beautiful girl with dark hair, her toned dancer's calves peeking out from under her skirt. Karen DiPlacido walked into the room each morning smiling and laughing, her raspy voice filling the room. My Catholic school, Mercyhurst Preparatory, determined the homerooms alphabetically by last name, so I was in the A–D class with Karen DiPlacido, the last person to make the alphabetical cut-off.

At the time, I didn't care about dance, but I made an exception whenever Karen performed. When she was in the school dance performance, I strategically snagged a seat in the front.

My friend Craig dared me to ask her out.

"No way." I was too nervous.

Craig and I played on the soccer and basketball teams together. The school planned to add football the next year, which would allow me to resume my NFL pursuit.

We studied and went to practice hoping to land an athletic scholarship. Neither of us drank. We were rule followers.

Karen was a rule breaker. She spent her time with the "party kids."

After freshman year, Karen and I were no longer in the same homeroom. Gone as well was the school's plan to add a football team. They said it would have to wait due to budget reasons. I was devastated. How could I play in the NFL someday if I didn't even play football in high school?

Watching NFL games on Sunday, I had a spark of an idea. I saw the rosters littered with former soccer players. One in particular, Morten

Andersen from Denmark, played just one year of football in high school and was the best kicker in the league.

One year, zero years. What's the difference? I thought. I would just train myself to kick on the side and then walk on to a Division I football team when I got to college. Problem solved.

Walk-ons are college football's dreamers. They're athletes who are neither recruited nor offered scholarships and instead try out for the team. I learned only recently that just 6 percent of those who play football in high school go on to play at the collegiate level, Division III included. Of the almost 70,000 who play in college, only 300 will make an NFL roster each year. Of the over one million kids playing high school football right now, more than 99 percent will *never* play in the NFL.

I started spending my extra time walking to the field with a ball under my arm and a tee in my pocket. It was a 10-minute walk past my friends' houses, past the homes from my old paper route, around the corner past the old church, then through the high school parking lot. An eight-foot-tall chain-link fence enclosed the field, and a gravel track circled it. The field featured more stones and dirt than grass. I usually found myself alone there, with the occasional exception of a runner jogging along the track.

I loved team sports. I found that an unexpected benefit of playing sports year-round was that it channeled and even eased my ADD. The physical exertion gave me an outlet to release energy and a way to calm my mind.

But it was kicking a ball through the uprights that gave me the most joy. There was something calming about training alone. I wasn't getting in trouble. I was just having fun. I wasn't competing or trying to prove anything to anyone.

My racing mind became immersed in play in the moment. I could kick for hours, sometimes until the sun went down. I would reach down, pick up a handful of grass, and let the wind take it away to see the direction it was blowing that day. I loved the smell of the grass. I loved watching the ball sail through the air, flying end over end through the goalposts with just the sky for a background. I would imagine lining up for a last-second field goal in front of a roaring crowd—and then splitting the uprights.

"The crowd goes wild!" There in the damp, sparse grass, with the sun sinking behind the trees, it was my own field of dreams.

I never thought about the impossible odds because for me, it was 100 percent that I would play in the NFL. I simply couldn't envision anything else. I was a kicker. It's just who I was, and who I would always be.

In the spring of my senior year, our basketball season ended with a thud. We were knocked out of the district playoffs on a last-second shot right in front of my face. I couldn't stop thinking of the shot. It replayed and looped in my mind. Why couldn't I have blocked his shot? It was my fault our season was over. My obsession to win was sometimes my downfall. After losses, I felt worthless and humiliated, as if my whole existence depended on the scoreboard.

With no sports to play, and to keep myself busy and free my mind from thinking about the end of my high school sports career, I decided to attend a youth group. There was buzz from my friends about a young deacon at Our Lady of Peace Church.

As I entered the church, I told myself to keep a low profile. The community room was swarming with about three-dozen high school kids. A man who looked to be in his 20s with dark hair and a bounce in his walk strutted across the room, attention focused on me like a tractor beam.

"Nice to meet you, pagan!" *Pagan? What is this guy's problem?* The whole room had heard him, and everyone was looking at me.

He had a booming voice and an accent that I couldn't place. I later discovered it was Pittsburghese, in which vowels are shortened so that the Pittsburgh Steelers become the "Stillers" and iron is pronounced "arn." He extended his hand and gave mine a hard squeeze while he looked me in the eye with a mischievous smirk.

Larry had grown up in the rough-and-tumble North Side of Pittsburgh. His parents were Pittsburgh city cops.

After some group exercises, Larry gave us a short talk before the session ended.

"Did you do at least one act of unselfishness today?" he asked us. "If the answer is no, then you squandered the whole day on yourself."

His body swayed and his hands moved constantly, showing his Italian upbringing.

I tried to tune him out.

"Sean, I'm talking to you!"

There were 30 other kids in the room. Why was he picking on me? What was his problem?

What did I get myself into? I didn't need this. After about two months, I stopped going. I didn't need this. I figured it would be the last I saw of Larry. I was wrong.

• • •

In Erie, Catholic schools and churches seemed to be everywhere. Our Lady of Peace, Our Lady Christian, St. Luke's, St. Paul's, St. Andrew's, and so on. Our high school, Mercyhurst Prep, was Catholic. I assumed that people's dogs, cats, and goldfish were Catholic. Our family went to church together every week.

Our principal was open-minded. My senior year, she taught a class called Religions of the World, where we learned about Buddhism, and that Buddha was not as chubby as many representations of him would make it appear. He was depicted that way because fleshiness was symbolic of happiness in the East. We discovered that in Hinduism, karma is the universal principle of cause and effect, and through the lessons of life, one can become a better person. She told us that the social activist and boxer Muhammad Ali had once been Cassius Clay, and that *Islam* was an Arabic word that meant peace. We listened to a talk by a survivor from Auschwitz that brought us to tears and woke us up to the realities of anti-Semitism.

There were only six people in this class, and one of them was Karen. For the last few years, the best I could do with her had been an uneasy smile in the hallway. Now, I got to sit behind her and stare at her the whole class while the teacher talked about the Buddha meditating under the Bodhi tree.

I thought someone had thrown me a softball when I ended up in that class. All I had to do was swing the bat. But there was just one wrinkle in my game plan. She had a boyfriend. Kyle. He had David Bowie spiked hair and a white Corvette with nice rims and a thumping stereo. Karen had played Patty Simcox in the school musical *Grease*, while he'd played

Sonny, a gang member of the T-Birds, in a white T-shirt and black leather jacket. How could I compete with that? I got my hair cut at Sal's Barber Shop on the lower east side of town with my dad. Each time, they'd give me a look even nerdier than the one before. One week, it was *party in the front* and *business in the back*. The next visit, they'd give me a Mr. Spock bowl cut.

One afternoon, the teacher announced a field trip: We were all invited to her cottage on the lake to watch the movie *Gandhi*. I knew a right-over-the-plate pitch when I saw one. I offered Karen a ride. Now, I didn't have my own car. My father let me drive our brown '78 Toyota station wagon, which was dotted with cigarette burns, rocked only AM radio, and smelled like a mixture of cheese and our pine tree air freshener. Not exactly the ideal dating mobile, but it moved from A to B. It would have to do.

Out we went, the two of us, with her friend Lisa and my 6-foot-2 basketball buddy Anton, who could dunk like Michael Jordan. On the drive to the cabin, Karen flirted with me, flipping my Cleveland Indians baseball hat, changing the dials on the radio, messing with my windshield wipers, blasting the heat, and poking fun at me and Anton. I liked her from afar, but I loved her more close up.

A few days later, Karen invited me over to her mother's apartment to study with her for the final exam. She was her usual self: laughing and playful. There were unopened boxes sitting on the floor and no pictures on the wall. When I asked what was up with that, she informed me that a couple of weeks earlier her mom had decided to move out and separate from her father. I asked her if she was okay.

She lifted her head from her notebook and gazed at me with her dark eyes. "I try not to think about it. I'm trying to keep myself busy. I go out a lot. I run every day. I feel embarrassed, but I know I shouldn't."

Her eyes welled up.

"But people make such a big deal about divorce. My mom is a Eucharistic minister at St. Andrew's, she hands out the hosts on Sundays, but now that she is getting a divorce, she has to quit."

My parents were together. It was out of my depth. I didn't understand divorce. But I wanted to hug her.

I changed the topic. "Do you know where you are going to college?"

"Yeah, I want to go far away. I even applied to Alaska. If I had my way, I would go to New York City and become a Broadway dancer. But my mom told me yesterday I'm going to Edinboro." This was a town 20 minutes south of Erie. "I have no choice. My uncle is the basketball coach there, so I can go for almost nothing. But I'm not going to stay there. I have big dreams. I just don't know exactly what they are yet."

She asked me my plans. I told her that a few small schools recruited me for basketball and soccer and I would play soccer in college.

I couldn't tell her that I was kicking field goals every chance I got, hoping to play for a big college.

I didn't share my Division I and NFL dream with her because I was afraid of what she would think. But at least I found out we had more in common than I first thought. We were both dreamers. I was just too scared to share mine.

• • •

I tried to keep the NFL dream to myself; my dad was the only one I told. I feared telling anyone else, assuming they would think my idea was ridiculous. But one day, I shared my secret plan with some of my friends at lunch. Craig, who was the master at pushing my buttons, laughed in my face.

"Cons, you don't even play football in high school. How are you going to play in college? You're high," he said, laughing.

I told him that I kicked by myself on the weekends and sometimes after soccer practice. He didn't buy it. "What good will that do?"

It was a logical and fair question. But even though my friends and I made a semiprofessional sport out of making fun of each other, it set me on fire.

"You're a fucking asshole!" I stood up and launched a hard pretzel at his face from point-blank range across the table. Direct hit to the forehead. Unbeknownst to him, a chunk of it remained lodged in his skin for the rest of the lunch period.

Maybe Craig was right. Who dreams of playing in the NFL but doesn't play football in high school? It sounded crazy.

But at the same time, another voice in my head insisted on ignoring that thought. I had spent hours *doing what I loved*, and I knew I was good at it, even if no one but my dad ever saw me do it.

The time came to select a college. Instead of walking on at a Division I school such as Pitt or Notre Dame, I decided it was best to first get experience at a nearby Division III school and then transfer to a big school later.

Like most kids from Erie, my parents told me my choices were limited to schools in Pennsylvania no more than two hours away that they could afford. I chose the school that I was most familiar with, Grove City College, a tiny conservative Christian school less than an hour and a half from my family's home. I had visited the school only once, for a soccer camp. It was a Division III program and they couldn't offer scholarships. They gave plenty of financial aid, and I just needed the green light from the football coach that I could walk on.

I gave the head coach, Coach Smith, a call to ask him if I could join the team. "Where did you play in high school?" he asked me.

"I didn't. I played soccer and basketball. But I trained as a kicker at a field."

Silence.

"When was the last time you were on a football team?"

"Eighth grade."

More silence.

He finally responded and told me I could join the team on the first day of classes.

When I told my parents of my decision, they thought I was confused. They suggested I go the safe route and play soccer or basketball at one of the other small schools that recruited me. They mentioned I could join the service like my father and so many other kids in Erie who didn't know what to do with their lives. But I insisted I knew exactly what I wanted. I was a kicker.

At high school graduation in May 1988, I sat up tall and swayed, trying to get a clear view of Karen walking on the stage. There she was in her gown, hair flowing out of her cap. My eyes fixed on her as she walked back to her seat, smiling the whole way.

That evening at a friend's graduation party, I walked down into the basement. Michael Jackson's *Bad* album was blasting on the stereo.

Standing next to the wall in a black-and-white dress was Karen.

She came over and gave me a hug.

"Let's sit here." She motioned to a beat-up velour armchair in the corner.

I looked at her awkwardly as it was big enough for only one person.

She bumped me and said, "Here, sit." In an instant, I was in the chair, and she sat on my lap, crossed her legs, and put her arm behind me.

We laughed and flirted until the party ended around midnight, when we hugged goodbye.

It was the last time I saw her for a while.

I spent the summer working as a delivery driver for a pizza shop to help pay for college and obsessively kicked, ran, and lifted weights. I was ready for the next step of my dream.

CHAPTER 3
SIDELINED

tossed my suitcase filled with clothes, a duffel bag with cleats and footballs, and a cardboard box stocked with licorice, chips, and Cheez-Its into the trunk of my parents' car, and we rolled 75 minutes south on Interstate 79. It was a hot day in mid-August 1988. My parents helped move me into Grove City, a tiny college of about two thousand students. They gave me goodbye hugs, and then off they went back to Erie.

I was assigned to a nether region of the West Dormitory known as the Mole Hole, a dimly lit single hallway of 20 boys' double rooms illogically located in the basement of the girls' dorm. My hallmates and I were convinced that our sock-smelling cave was where the college housed its undesirables, students who'd gotten in by the skin of their teeth.

At freshman orientation, we were supplied with chapel cards, which needed to be handed in at chapel to prove we had gone 16 times a semester. The rule when we had a female companion in the room was "a shoe in the door and a foot on the floor at all times." There was no alcohol allowed on campus, and the town was dry. This was news to me. I must have missed it in the college guidebook.

Once orientation wrapped up, it was time to see the football coach. When I got to the football office, there was no coach, just a young girl sitting at a desk in a crimson polo shirt, who looked at me blankly when I said I was on the team.

She told me my name wasn't on the roster and to come back the next day. I figured it was just a miscommunication.

The next day, I waited in the lobby. After about 20 minutes, coaches dressed in their tan khakis and crimson polo shirts started filing out. I spotted Coach Smith. I introduced myself and reminded him of our phone conversation.

"I'm sorry," he said, "We already have a kicker."

My body shook as I reminded him again that he told me I could join the team.

He told me, "Sorry, we don't need another kicker." And he walked away.

The walk back to my room along the pathways in the quad with manicured grass and neo-Gothic buildings always looked so idyllic to me. But that day, I wanted to get as far away from there as possible. I walked past kids with backpacks and professors in bowties, but I didn't see them.

I sat alone on a bench in the quad. I was marooned on a dry college campus with nothing but a church punch card and no football in my future.

Maybe this dream is dumb. I envisioned Craig with that pretzel embedded in his forehead, laughing at me, and I thought maybe he was right. Why would I ever have thought I could just start playing organized football at the age of 18 and be successful at it?

I called my dad for some advice.

"Why don't you ask the soccer coach if he'll let you join the team? He sent you a letter after he saw you play in camp."

"But the season already started."

"What do you have to lose?"

The head coach remembered me from summer camp and let me join the team, which was some consolation, but something was missing for me on the soccer field. My eyes were continually drawn to the football team on the adjacent field. I watched the kickers practicing near the goalposts, and I couldn't let it go. I needed to kick.

My father had taught me to give my all in everything and never quit. But I felt I wasn't being fair to the soccer team. I knocked on my coach's door.

He took one look at me.

"Let me guess," he said. "You're quitting, aren't you?"

Without soccer, all I had was class, mandatory chapel (which I dreaded), and my friends in the underground prison. I had to go somewhere else. Where? I hadn't a clue. But not here.

At least my studies were engaging. I was fascinated by Philosophy 101, which was taught by the president of the college. We learned the Socratic method and the Socratic paradox, "I know that I know nothing." My history professor told stories about the adversity that George Washington faced. He nearly drowned in the icy waters of the Allegheny River. His ragtag soldiers lost multiple battles against the British. He lost over and over. But he possessed tenacity, persistence, and he learned from his failures.

The professors' lectures interested me and took me to another place and time, but when it came time to take tests, my ADD got the best of me. I got hammered by the exams, which were heavy on writing. I had a hard time stringing together clear thoughts on paper. All I thought about was, where could I play football?

The D+ I earned in philosophy was my best grade that first semester. I got a D in history, and it looked like my college life was about to become history, too.

One weekend in December, near the end of my first semester, I got an invite from some old high school friends who were freshmen at Kent State University, about an hour and a half west, across the border in Ohio. I asked my friends Bill and Kevin if they were up for a road trip. "Let's get out of here! I'm going nuts," Kevin said.

It was the usual college visit: We partied all day long and into the night. Around 2:00 a.m., Bill thought it was best that we head back to school. I was already eight to 10 drinks deep, but I always felt invincible behind the wheel, even when drunk, so I offered to drive.

We were about half an hour into the ride when it began to snow giant flakes. It was the Christmas season, and I found the local all-Christmas radio station, which was featuring my favorite, Andy Williams. We started belting out "It's the Most Wonderful Time of the Year," "Rudolph the Red-Nosed Reindeer," "Silent Night," etc. Not satisfied with our vocal volume alone, I started moving the windshield wipers in time with the rhythm. Then I really took our mobile holiday party to the next level, turning the headlights on and off in sync with the wipers. For some mysterious reason, our vehicle attracted the attention of an Ohio state trooper.

He made his first appearance in my rearview mirror outside Canfield, Ohio, near Youngstown. Then, I got to meet him in person on the side of the road.

"Do you know why I pulled you over?" he asked.

I wanted to say, *You don't like Andy Williams?*

"Step out of the car, son."

He held a pen in front of my eyes and moved it back and forth. "We got a sleepy driver," he snapped to his partner.

Then he asked me to walk in a straight line.

"We got a drunk one, too."

We caught a ride in the back of his cruiser. At the station, I failed the Breathalyzer test, and while my friends caught some shut-eye in the lobby, I spent the night down the hall in a jail cell. The next morning, they let Bill drive us home, but I was ordered to appear in court in Ohio a few weeks later for sentencing. Since I was 18, my parents weren't notified. I was relieved. I promised myself to never get behind the wheel while drunk again.

When I made it back to school, the campus was covered in snow. It looked beautiful, and everyone was getting excited about Christmas. But I didn't see any reason to be excited about anything.

I started skipping classes. I spent a lot of time just lying in bed staring at the ceiling while my roommate, who thought he was Tom Petty, played his guitar and sang like he was giving birth. I needed to get out of there. After class, when I went out, I walked into Grove City. The town had little more than a diner, drugstore, and hardware store. I went by myself to see movies at the 60-year-old Guthrie Theater, where an antique yellow-and-maroon sign on the marquee advertised *Die Hard* and *Who Framed Roger Rabbit.*

I was anxious about my upcoming January court appearance. Would it go on my record? Would I have to serve jail time? Would no other school ever accept me? I would see Coach Smith at times walking through campus, and the sight of him reminded me that my future was nothing without football.

I applied to the one and only college in Erie with a football team, Mercyhurst. When the letter arrived a couple weeks later, it read, "Thank you for your interest in Mercyhurst College. After careful consideration, we regret to inform you . . ." A letter with a big red rejection stamp would have made it quicker.

I bombed my finals and ended the semester with a 1.33 GPA. I was embarrassed to go back to Erie and see my family and friends, but I didn't know where else to go. At the end of my first semester of college, I notified the school I would not be coming back in January. I quit school and moved back home.

• • •

A couple of weeks later, I headed out for my first day of work. I'd gotten a minimum-wage job at the local General Nutrition Center, better known as GNC. It was a 15-minute walk from my house, and I would walk there six days a week in the cold darkness of Erie winter mornings. I was 19. My friends were in college, seemingly having a ball, and there I was, a complete failure. Instead of calculus, the only equation I knew was "Me = Giant Loser."

Each day was as hard to get a handle on as a fog. I felt like I had no control of what came next. My mind drifted through gray fields of negative self-talk. *You'll never amount to anything*, said a voice in my head. If I couldn't play football, why bother? What else was there? I wanted another chance to prove I could be a football player.

My dream had imploded, and I was making it worse through self-hatred. I heard Coach Smith's words. *We don't need you.* I let my anger toward Coach Smith cloud my mind. I felt paralyzed, unable to take action. Depression seemed to knot itself around me. I didn't share my feelings with anyone; I just let them fester.

It was the unknown that I was afraid of. There would always be things I couldn't change. Things wouldn't always go my way. No matter how hard I tried, there would always be doubters.

Though I didn't know it at the time, those with ADD tend to blame themselves for everything because they have been conditioned to believe they are troublesome and problem makers.

To keep my self-talk from destroying me, I knew of one way. To kick. It was my medicine. It worked better than any pill for me.

After work each late afternoon, I walked home as fast as I could. Clouds usually blocked the light. I reminded myself that the sun was still up there. It was around 4:30, with just an hour of daylight left. I changed out of my work uniform and put on my long johns, sweatpants, and two long-sleeve shirts. I tossed my two worn footballs and tee into my ball bag, put on my cleats, winter hat, and gloves, grabbed a snow shovel, and hiked to the field.

The field was always covered with at least a foot of snow. In a rush against twilight, I kicked on top of the snow and ice. As I tried to find my footing, my kicks wobbled through the air. I grabbed my shovel and cleared a spot at what I guessed was the 30 yard line.

Each time, I was alone but never felt lonely. I would kick past sunset. But it was still light. The white snow glowed under the light of the moon. I kept kicking. I couldn't feel my toes. The ball felt like a brick when I kicked it. But the balls kept going through the uprights.

My confidence soared like the balls flying through the air. If I could make field goals in the most difficult of conditions, what could stop me on a warm fall day with fresh-cut grass? Confidence was a skill I was developing through repetition, focus, and effort.

Opponents and disbelievers were already against me, but I couldn't ever be against myself. I didn't fear failure. By practicing every day, I knew what I was capable of. I cultivated a faith and belief in my ability.

I realized that my so-called failure with the coach at Grove City was needed. I would continue to seek out challenges. I accepted that I would experience more failures in these challenges. But that would only strengthen my resilience and help me be the best I could be. Nothing could stop me. Not even my ADD.

At the end of January, my court date was coming up. It was set for 8:00 a.m. on a Monday in Youngstown, Ohio—about a two-hour drive from Erie. But I wasn't allowed to drive in Ohio, so I needed a ride. Out of desperation, I called Deacon Larry.

"Hey pagan," he said, when I told him who it was.

"I got in a little trouble down at school."

"You got a DUI, didn't you?"

I said that I had to go to court the following Monday. In Ohio. And that no, I hadn't told my mom and dad; they'd kill me.

I asked him for a ride, and he said yes.

I asked Deacon Larry to pick me up at 5:30 a.m. in an abandoned grocery store parking lot 10 blocks from my house. I slipped out of the house and made the walk on the ice-covered sidewalks, wondering if this guy was really going to do this for me. Who would get up at five in the morning, drive some punk kid two hours to court, sit there all day, pay a fine, and then drive the idiot back home?

I stood alone in the lifeless parking lot while a handful of street-lights flickered and a gentle snow fell. At 5:35, a lone pair of headlights appeared through the blackness. A blue car slowed, pulled into the lot, and approached me. The window rolled down a crack.

It was Larry.

I struggled to come up with conversation on the two-hour ride over the pitch-black highways of the Midwest. I questioned him on the role of a deacon and the differences between a deacon and a priest. Snow was piled high along the sides of the road. Along the highway, the only lights came from random houses that still had their Christmas lights up.

We rolled into Youngstown, driving past manufacturing plants and into the old downtown, where we found the county courthouse. We were instructed to have a seat on a wooden bench in the hallway until my name was called. After an hour, they called me in. The officer who pulled me over was there, sitting in the first row of the courtroom. I just wanted to get it over with.

The judge asked me if I had an attorney. I told them no. "But I'm here with Deacon Larry," I said, thinking that might help my chances especially since he was wearing his collar.

The judge read out loud the charges and some of the details of the night.

"How do you plead?" he asked.

"Guilty."

"I sentence you to five days in an alcohol rehab and education clinic and a fine of $400. You are not permitted to drive in the state of Ohio for twelve months."

This sounded fair to me. Guess I wouldn't be transferring to Ohio State though.

We found an old-fashioned roadside diner on the way home and were seated in the red pleather booth near the jukebox. I'd begun to feel more at ease with Larry. A man with a black shirt and collar was not who I had pictured I would be hanging out with when I was a freshman, but I had no one else.

As we drove home past the snow-laced barren cornfields, with the dreaded court date behind me, the quiet day and our conversation brought me some clarity. I knew it was time to try something different.

I asked him to drop me off at the vacant parking lot a safe distance from my house to complete the undercover operation. As we approached the lot, he offered to pay my fine, on the condition I pay him back over the course of a year. I agreed. And one more thing: "I'm becoming a priest in three months. You're going to serve my first mass."

I tried to wiggle out of it by telling him that when I was an altar boy in grade school, I stole two pounds of hosts.

"Good, now you can make up for it," he said. "April 21, Our Lady of Peace Church."

Before I shut the door, I asked him, "Are you into racquetball? Do you want to meet at my gym tomorrow?" Something told me I could use a friend right now.

I walked home, and when my parents asked me why I'd been gone so long, I told them I'd had a long day at work. I always had the option to go to confession to be absolved for my lie.

The next morning, in a best of three, I beat Larry mercilessly 15–2 and 15–1. I hit the ball so hard off the walls that he was running, diving, and ducking like he was playing dodgeball. Halfway through the first game, he appeared to be swearing under his breath, and his face resembled a soon-to-erupt volcano, Mount Larry. I was going straight to hell.

Back in the locker room, we didn't talk for about 10 minutes. Then Larry broke the awkward silence.

"How often do you work out?"

"Every day. Usually one to two hours at the gym plus I kick every day."

"How much time each day do you spend sitting quietly, meditating, praying, and listening?"

"About five minutes?" (I was rounding up from zero.) "What does this have to do with racquetball?" I asked.

"Everything!" he replied. "So you spend two hours a day beating the crap out of your body so you can have ripped abs, biceps, and be a kicker? And you spend only five minutes a day in silence listening?"

CHAPTER 4
MOVING THE GOALPOSTS

My father walked in as I was having breakfast and tossed the sports section of the *Erie Daily Times* on the table in front of me.

"Look at this."

The article announced that Gannon University, where my brother went to school, just 10 minutes from my house, would be starting a brand-new Division III football program that fall. I had to read the article a second time to believe it.

First thing on Monday morning, I borrowed my father's car and drove to downtown Erie. The lady in the admissions office handed me the application and I speed-walked over to the Erie Public Library a few blocks away. I borrowed a pen and some scrap paper from the librarian and found a tucked-away chair on the second floor and filled it out. An hour later, I was standing in front of the admissions lady again with application in hand.

She told me they'd be in touch within a month or two. I went back the next week to ask if they had made a decision. A few days later, I called them. A week later, I stopped by again. I soon knew the names of all the ladies in the office.

This was it. There was no backup plan. It was Gannon University or bust.

About 30 days after I'd dropped off the application, the letter showed up in the mailbox. The kind in the big envelope. Despite its size, I thought, *here it is. Another rejection.* I couldn't open it in front of my parents because I didn't want them to see my reaction if I got rejected *again*. So I went upstairs to our attic, my escape room.

I held the envelope up next to the window overlooking our backyard for light, and after turning it every which way to see through it, I saw the words, "We are excited to share with you . . ." I tore it open.

It came with a caveat, however. I had received a conditional acceptance. I had to keep my grades above a 2.0 in the first year, and if I did, they'd let me come back the next year.

Early in the summer before my enrollment, I made an appointment with Tom Herman, the coach who'd be resurrecting a program that had not competed in football since 1950. Coach Herman and his "in-the-works" staff occupied the fourth floor of a downtown office building three blocks from campus. When I exited the elevator, a Xeroxed "Gannon Football" sign pointed me in the right direction. The offices consisted of sparsely outfitted cubicles where unopened boxes graced the empty desks. But there seemed to be no one around. *Oh shit*, I thought. *Not again.* Then a tall lady in a blue dress appeared around the corner.

"Hi, are you Sean?" she said. "Coach Herman is on his way."

Out of nowhere, like a wizard it seemed, came Coach Herman, sporting a maroon Gannon Football golf shirt and a Coppertone-tan face. He stood about an inch taller than me and had the look of a worn, retired football player as he walked with a slight limp. He gave me a firm handshake and invited me to have a seat in his office.

"Tell me about yourself," he said, leaning forward over his desk. "And why you want to play football for Gannon."

How long did he have? I told him about my athletic past and that I had not played in high school but had been practicing kicking on the side for years and that if given a chance I knew I could help the team.

"We're brand-new to this, too," he said. "I've never even been a head coach before. This school hasn't had a team since the end of World War II. We don't have a practice field yet. But we'll get one by August. We have just three coaches on staff right now including myself, but we'll be ready come training camp."

He was an underdog. Just like me. He had something to prove.

He jumped out from behind his desk and wrapped his arm around me and squeezed me like a bear.

"I don't give a horse's ass that you've never played before. Everyone who wants to play is gonna get a chance to show how they can help the team."

I couldn't believe my ears. I had found a home.

• • •

The afternoon before the first day of training camp, I walked into the house. It was the middle of August. I had just finished kicking about 50 balls at the field. My dad was working second shift, 2:00 to 10:00 p.m. Today, he was going to let me drive him to work, so I could drop him off and then go to the gym to get in one last workout before training camp.

In the kitchen, I saw my dad's usual lunch bag and his white plastic bag with the drawstring. A maroon-and-gold magazine peeking out from the top caught my eye. I pulled it out. It was the Gannon football preview magazine. I wondered why my dad never told me he had it. He usually shared all his sports magazines with me. I flipped through the pages. It talked about the upcoming inaugural season and the projected players for the offense, defense, and special teams (which included the kickers). I turned to the last section and saw that the kicker would be a kid named Scott Price, a transfer from Mercyhurst, and his competition was a kicker named Kevin Rowland from a local Erie high school.

My dad didn't want me to see that I was discounted again. But it only strengthened my resolve. I felt jolted back to the reminder that I would have competition, but I wouldn't let it distract me. No matter whom I competed against, if I kicked to the best of my ability, I would be the starting kicker.

Everyone on the team was new. Most of the kids were freshmen, 18 or 19 years old. Most were from western Pennsylvania: steel mill towns, coal towns, farm towns, oil towns, mining towns, and some city boys from Pittsburgh and Erie.

The "facility" was an abandoned Catholic seminary that the university rented. We disembarked from the buses to get our first look at our spartan home for the next few weeks. It was perched on a wooded hillside, formerly a home for aspiring priests and deacons. We took turns going through the equipment stations, getting fitted by the managers: shoulder pads, pants, and then the helmets. Once we got the correct size helmet with the right facemask, they instructed us to grab the masking tape. "Write your name on the tape and put it on the front of the helmet so the coaches know who you are."

I laced up my scuffed soccer shoe and slid my right foot into it. It fit like a glove. As I put my shoe on the left foot, the laces broke. I tied the world's tiniest knot, and then I noticed the hard plastic bottom was peeling off the shoe.

"Do you have any black cleats? I just need one for my left foot. Size 12."

The equipment manager found me a shoe to wear. It didn't match, but it would have to do.

Outside the makeshift locker room, in a hall that led to the field, the coaches had posted the depth chart for every position. Players were ranked top to bottom. If you had a number one next to your name, you were the starter; number two meant you were the backup; and number three was third string. The kickers' list read Price, Rowland, Sopher, Conley. Last. Fourth string. I absorbed it, pictured my name on the top, and then kept moving.

There were over 80 of us of varying sizes and shapes. We scattered about the field and warmed up. The quarterbacks passed back and forth and the linemen stretched on the ground, while the running backs jogged in zigzag patterns.

There was just one goalpost. Sort of. I spotted a makeshift H-shaped steel structure on motorcycle wheels nestled up next to the woods. I walked toward the goalposts and saw three kickers with their helmets off lying on the field stretching. Scott Price, the starter, told us that Coach Comer wanted us to roll the goalposts over to the north end of the field and do some warmup kicks.

Special teams coach Pat Comer emerged from the locker room.

All I knew of him was what I had read in his bio in that magazine in my dad's bag. Thirty years old, Coach Comer had played for the Erie Express in the late 70s and for the Twin City Cougars of the California Professional League in the early 80s. He was a throwback, a player from the days when the kicker would kick the ball with his toe in a style known as "straight on." By the time I was playing in college, we kicked from the side, or "soccer style." Since his playing days, Coach Comer had put on some weight that found a home in his cheeks, and he sported a thick 'stache.

"Okay, ladies, let's start with some short field goals from the 20 yard line. Take two kicks each. Go in the order of the depth chart. Scott, you go first."

Scott was on a first-name basis with the coach already. He'd been his kicker in high school at Coach Comer's previous job. He also had college game experience. He was a transfer from Mercyhurst, where he'd made eight kicks the year before. Like Coach Comer, he was a straight-on kicker. He wore a special shoe that had a square toe like the head of a hammer.

After Scott kicked a half-dozen toe balls, Rowland went, then Sopher. They both kicked soccer style. "Does everyone now kick like a fairy soccer player?" Coach Comer asked.

While we kicked, we encouraged each other. But it was fake. We all wanted to be the starter. Coach Comer would squeeze in a jab before each one of us took our turn. He was trying to fluster us. I didn't pay attention when the other kickers went. I kept imagining myself making my kicks.

"You're up, Conley," Coach Comer said.

I lined up to kick by taking my customary three steps back and two steps to the left. The holder, Mike, a backup quarterback, held the ball in place with his index finger. I gazed at the ball and locked onto the spot where I would strike it with my foot.

"Conley, you look like a homeless person in those two different cleats," Comer said to me. Scott burst out laughing. I pretended to laugh to show it didn't bother me.

I looked toward the goalposts and noticed the tennis courts about 20 yards beyond the goalposts. The courts were protected with a giant chain-link fence about 20 feet high. Two couples were engaged in a friendly game. An ideal landing spot.

I struck the ball. It soared above the goalposts and skimmed over the high fence and landed with a thud on the tennis court to the shock of the retired couples.

Coach Comer looked at me in bewilderment. Scott was no longer laughing and had his mouth wide open. I felt everyone staring at me. My next two kicks landed in the court as well.

Comer, with his hands on his hips, turned to the other kickers. "Tomorrow, I just want to see Scott and Conley kick. No more turns for you guys. And Conley, go get the fucking balls out of the tennis court."

• • •

One night, there was a knock on my dorm room door. On the other side was Scott, the other kicker. My nemesis. Coach's pet. "Conley. Coach Comer wants to see you. He's in room 212."

The coaches stayed in the dorms with us during training camp. They claimed it was for team bonding, but it was mainly so they could babysit us. When I walked into Coach Comer's room at the end of the second-floor hallway, Scott was standing up against the wall with his arms crossed and a smirk on his face. Coach Comer was sitting in his desk chair with beads of sweat on his forehead. He told me to have a seat.

"Dude," he said to me. "Why are you here?"

"Um," I stuttered. "I want to play football? Be on a team."

"No, I mean why are you *here* at Gannon, a start-up Division III, and not at a Division I school like Notre Dame, Penn State, or Pitt? I was a kicker myself in a semi-pro league. I've seen a lot of kickers in my time, including some that made it to the NFL. And you're the best damn kicker I've ever seen. Do you know you could play in the NFL someday?"

There was a long pause. A surge of adrenaline coursed through me. Coach Comer was the first coach to believe in me. I knew I was good. It felt pretty good to hear someone else say it though.

"I'm going to help you get to the NFL," he continued. "I'm naming you the starting kicker. I'm not crazy about your weird soccer style. But, it works for you." He gestured toward Scott. "Scott will be the starting punter. I don't think you realize how fucking good you are. Get yourself some matching cleats. Go see the equipment manager tomorrow and tell him what you need."

I was conflicted. Finally someone else believed in my dream. Yet, I had a secret. I wanted to get to a bigger school to showcase my talents. At the same time, I couldn't ditch the first football coach to believe in me. What if the next coach didn't?

Our first game was against Iona College in New Rochelle, New York. This would be Gannon University's first football game in almost 40 years, and everyone was jumpy. The team made the seven-hour drive, and I was nervous as shit to play my first-ever game in front of a crowd—and in front of my parents, who had made the trek to watch me. I prayed I wouldn't let my team and Coach Comer down. The locker room was eerily quiet before the game. It was freshmen and a few sophomores versus an experienced full team of upperclassmen who were bigger and faster. *How bad would they beat us tonight?* we wondered.

The early September game kicked off at 7:00 under the stadium lights with the summer warmth still clinging to the grass. We wore brand-new white uniforms with maroon-and-gold stripes and letters. Early in the game, our offense was driving toward the end zone and we had the ball deep into their side of the field. But the drive stalled on the 14 yard line. It was fourth down.

"Field goal team!" Coach Herman called.

Out we came. I was setting up for a 31-yard field goal attempt. Thirty-one yards is considered easy for college kickers, a chip shot. It was a kick I had made thousands of times in practice and on my neighborhood field, and typically the ball would land at least 30 yards beyond the goalposts. There were no more than a thousand people in the stands, but the pressure made it feel like a hundred thousand.

I took my three steps back and two steps to the left. My body shook. My legs felt like they were going to collapse. I thought, *there is no way I can kick this ball in this condition.* I pleaded with my legs, *stop shaking.* But all eyes were on me. I looked into the eyes of my holder and gave him the nod that I was ready, even though I wasn't. In football, there's no room to say, "Hey everyone, I just need a moment to calm down. Be with you shortly." *Hike!* The ball came back and my holder, Mike, placed it on the grass. I kicked the ball with a gentle patter instead of kicking it. It was all I could do.

It seemed like the ball was in the air forever, turning end over end. Finally, it cleared the goalposts by six inches. The referees put up their hands with the "It's good" sign. My holder gave me a man hug, and there were high fives all around.

Coach Comer greeted me on the sideline. "Man, that kick fucking sucked, but it doesn't matter. It still counts. Three points!" And he gave me a bear hug.

I had gotten my first kick in the books. It was a horrible kick, but it still counted, and it was over. I could exhale. After practically shitting my pants, I told myself, *I can't let this happen again if I'm ever going to be on the big stage. I need to relax.*

The team was outmatched and we lost 34–9.

That was the last field goal I would successfully make all season. I missed the next seven, to finish the season with a record of one out of eight.

It felt like I had no control over my swing. Instead of rotating end over end in the air, my balls would sometimes fly horizontal rotating like a helicopter blade. I had to conquer this.

How could I gain confidence when all I did was miss? I had to get over it. Michael Jordan missed free throws, Wayne Gretzky missed shots on goal. Or maybe it wasn't confidence. Maybe it was a technical glitch. Maybe I was trying too hard. There was only one way I knew to bounce back. Keep kicking. Try harder. There had to be a way that I could achieve perfection.

We lost every game. Our final record was 0-7. We lost our last game of the season 7–6 to Catholic University, because I missed an extra point that would have tied the game. An extra point is just 20 yards from the goalposts. It's considered automatic. In my mind, I'd lost the game for my team. I thought about that easy miss all winter, spring, and summer. I couldn't wait to get back onto the field. All offseason, I obsessed about how to be more precise.

Confidence is the most important quality a kicker can possess, more important than talent, health, conditioning, and endurance. It's the intangible. It separates the good kickers from great kickers. It's the thing that makes you able to bounce back after a miss. To make a last-second kick.

Making kicks builds confidence. Missing kicks takes it away. Missing short kicks or with the game on the line can be career crushing. Making a big kick can be career propelling.

Despite my terrible stats, I was still much better than the other kickers. So I was never in danger of losing my job. It was the inconsistency that was maddening for me, but it didn't seem to bother Coach Comer. I would crush a 40-yard field goal that would land 25 yards behind the goalposts, but then I would miss an extra point, just 20 yards away.

"You have to miss a bunch of kicks and then you'll make one and then you'll make another and then another," Comer told me. "And then you will be unstoppable. And then one day, you'll be playing on Sundays in the NFL."

I had to learn how to lose in order to know how to win.

My classes came easier than making field goals. Being on the team gave me the structure I needed. In the back of my mind, I kept thinking that if I got more consistent at making field goals I could still transfer to a Division I school. One out of eight kicks made in the season gave me a 12.5 percent success rate, which put me at the bottom of all Division III kickers in the country. Not exactly Division I material. To be a Division I kicker, 65 percent was the minimum expectation. It didn't seem out of reach.

I would also need solid grades to transfer, so I studied hard. I had a B average, two letters better than I had at Grove City.

• • •

Eight months after I missed the extra point against Catholic, I was back in training camp, watching the news with my roommate John. Tom Brokaw was telling us that a country I had never heard of, Iraq, had invaded the tiny country of Kuwait, starting the Gulf War.

Just then, Coach Comer barged in. "Hey girls. Sean, I need to talk to you. Let's go outside. It's too fucking hot in here. And your room smells like old pizza and farts."

We walked outside the dorm and sat on the steps.

"You're a junior now. This is the year you need to get on the radar for the NFL," he said. He paused, and then continued, "You must have worked hard in the offseason. You're bigger and stronger."

I looked him straight in the eye. It was true; I'd worked hard.

"Forget about last season. If you can kick the ball straight regularly and make most of your field goals this year, I can contact some NFL scouts. This is going to be your big year."

A couple of weeks later, in September, we played Hobart College, a small school from New York's Finger Lakes region. The game was held in our home stadium, Erie Veterans Memorial Stadium. It was used by all the local high schools on Friday evenings. Those games sometimes drew full capacity, which was 10,000. Today, we had our usual crowd of about a thousand—and that was counting the cheerleaders, ushers, janitors, and the men selling the hot dogs.

We were still looking for our first victory since October 1950.

I remembered Coach Comer's words. I needed a big year. Therefore, I needed some big games. The team was amped up before the game. We were getting hungry and angry.

On an early drive, we stalled at Hobart's 20 yard line. Coach Herman called for the field goal team. I crushed a 37-yarder that flew far beyond the goalposts. Later in the game, I made another one, this time from 39 yards. My kickoffs all found the end zone. Our young team pulled off the impossible. We won 20–10. One of the local TV stations interviewed me and Coach Herman after the game. He rubbed the top of my head while praising my performance to the sportscaster. This was more like it.

But what goes up, must come down. Near the end of the season, we played Duquesne University at South Side Stadium in Pittsburgh. The aging stadium, with its cement and metal bleachers, was enclosed by concrete walls and surrounded by a high chain-link fence, and had views of the downtown skyline.

I missed my first field goal that night wide right. Then my second wide right. Then my third wide left. Each kick flew higher than the top of the goalposts and traveled at least 60 yards.

I was like a drunken gardener with a spray hose.

When a kicker goes 0-for-3, that's bad. I had one more chance with just a few minutes left in the game. A total gimme, just 25 yards. Almost impossible to miss even if I kicked it with my left foot, but I was a complete head case at this point, and my level of confidence matched the number of field goals I had made, zero. I thought, *my teammates, coaches, and parents must think I suck.* I kicked. Shank. No good. 0-for-4.

As I jogged off the field and headed for the sideline, I did my best to find an area where there were no coaches. But they found me. I lowered my head as if looking for the nearest empty bench, hoping to bury my head like a turtle hiding in his shell. Both Coach Herman and Coach Comer did their best to tell me *it's okay.* But I had never felt more embarrassed. Standing by myself on the sidelines, I felt as if I was in solitary confinement. My confidence was shattered.

I dwelled on my misses. I let my ADD get the best of me. I tortured myself, reliving the misses. Compassionless. I tried to remind myself that I would never be a successful kicker if I dwelled on negative thoughts. Most of the players didn't say a word, but one told me that he envied my job during the practice week, but he didn't want it on game day.

I made just one more field goal that year. I finished the season 4 out of 8. In two years, I had made just five out of 16 field goals. According to the numbers, I was one of the worst kickers in the nation. My dream of playing Division I was looking dismal and making the NFL someday now seemed impossible.

I clung to the fact that my kickoffs and leg strength were good. I'd sometimes kick the ball through the entire end zone, which prevented the other team from running the ball back. I was the Happy Gilmore of kickers. I could kick the ball a country mile, but I still couldn't hit the side of a barn.

I started to think that *maybe* it would be best to do the safe thing and finish my college career at Gannon after all.

CHAPTER 5
RED ZONE

When my second season of college football ended in early December 1990, I got a job for a vending machine delivery company. After classes three days a week, I'd drive the eight-hour round-trip from Erie to Rochester, New York, often through the snow, in a white box truck piled high with pallets of Reese's Peanut Butter Cups, Cheetos, and canned Pepsi.

I was socking away as much money as possible, hoping to transfer soon, as I had only one year of college football eligibility left.

One of the characteristics of ADD is hyper-focusing. Single-mindedness. I was so intently focused on *getting there* that at times I didn't notice the world around me. I wouldn't stop pursuing my goal until I completed it.

While driving the truck, I spent hours lost in daydreams of playing for a Division I program. I hardly saw the road or heard the radio, I was so immersed in the future I wanted. My mind was in a constant state of struggle as two voices battled each other. One voice said, *Stay, it's safe and comfortable. You're the starting kicker, guaranteed. And what makes you think you should even try to get on a team at a Division I school? You play at the lowest level of college football, Division III. The statistics say you're one of the worst kickers in the country. Give it up.* The other voice said, *You have just one chance. You know you want it so bad. You've got to risk being devastated again to achieve your dream. If you fail again, you'll get back up. What if you worked harder and became so good, you became an NFL Hall of Famer one day?*

One day, on the way back from Rochester, dreaming of football and paying no attention to the gas nozzle in my hand, I filled my truck with gas. Forty-five minutes down the road, the fuel gauge needle started moving back and forth like it was possessed. Shit. I'd put in diesel fuel instead of unleaded. I'd ruined the engine.

I got off at the next exit and found a lone service station. I looked for a sign of life around the 1950s-style gas pump, scattered oil cans, and late-model rusted cars in the parking lot.

I went inside. A lanky, scruffy-faced attendant looked up in surprise.

"Hi," I said. "That's my truck out there. It runs on unleaded. I filled one of the tanks with diesel 50 miles back at the Angola rest stop. Is there anything I can do?"

"Bring your truck around back and I'll take care of it."

How was he going to get diesel gas *out* of the engine? I was eager to see that—it seemed impossible. With his mouth wrapped around the end of a hose, he sucked on it to get the diesel to start coming out, then placed the end of the hose into a rusty oil barrel so it could continue trickling out. When it was over, I thanked him. He replied, "All in a day's work." I gave him all the money in my pocket: $15.

I was able to drive the truck back to the warehouse, but it was too late. The diesel had already destroyed the engine—and the $30,000 truck. After I apologized, my boss, Mr. Stoddart, sitting at his desk stacked with invoices and bills, with his forehead wrinkled, said, "You can't do this job if you're going to be daydreaming behind the wheel."

He continued, "Take some time off." It was a nice way of firing me.

He was right. No more dreaming.

I didn't want to spend the rest of my life wondering whether I had given it my best shot.

About a week later, I went downtown to inform Coach Comer of my decision.

As I walked down the hall toward his office, my heart raced. My palms got sweaty. Each time I thought about turning around, I reminded myself the greater risk pursuing my dreams would be to do nothing. I didn't want to live with any regret.

"Coach, I want to thank you for everything you've done for me. You gave me a chance when no one else would. But I've decided to transfer to a D-I school next fall."

His eyes got bigger.

"What the fuck are you talking about?" The skin around his mustache contorted. There was an uncomfortable pause.

"If you stay and finish strong, you could be our first player to play in the NFL," he said.

I wanted to believe him, but I knew I would most likely never get noticed if I stayed. There were never NFL scouts in the stands or at practice and we were never on television. I knew of not a single kicker or any player that went from Division III to the NFL.

"Do you know how hard it is to walk on to a D-I school and start? You'll be going up against players on scholarships. And with your stats here, they may not even let you walk on."

He reminded me how according to NCAA rules, I would not be able to play next year as transfers were required to sit out a year to prohibit players from transferring wildly. And that would leave me with just one year to play, as a fifth-year senior.

"I just want you to know the odds you are going up against."

I told him I understood, but I still thought my best chance to make the NFL was to play at a bigger school. "I love Gannon but I get just one shot at this."

He settled back in his chair, and sighed. "I'm sad to see you go." I sensed that he thought I was going to fall flat on my face. I couldn't blame him. Everything he said about my odds was true.

Then he asked me where I was going to transfer.

"Notre Dame, Michigan, maybe Pitt. Whichever one needs a kicker the most."

He walked around his desk and gave me a hug. "Before you leave, go down to the equipment room. Tell them you need four brand-new footballs to train with over the summer. Good luck. If you change your mind, call me."

After our meeting, I walked up to the local drugstore and found my way to the magazine aisle: *People*, *Time*, *Newsweek*, *Seventeen*, and, finally, the sports magazines.

For three hours, I scanned the college football preview magazines, *Athlon*, and the *Sporting News*. I flipped through the pages and looked at the team rosters and statistics, hoping to find schools that appeared to be in need of a good kicker—maybe because their current kicker was graduating, or the kicker they had was struggling. Since I had just one more year of eligibility, I wanted to increase my chances of stepping right in as the starting kicker. Because I couldn't afford to buy the magazines, I sat on the dusty drugstore floor and scribbled notes on a piece of scrap paper until the clerk kicked me out. Then I went back the next day and picked up where I'd left off.

After a few days of studying page by page, team by team, I'd crossed off schools for various reasons: too hard to get into, too many kickers on scholarship, a returning All-American. Notre Dame. Off the list. Penn State. Off the list. The University of Pittsburgh, the cheapest and closest, had not just one but three kickers on scholarship, an impossible battle. Off the list. The remaining schools that fit my profile were Purdue, North Carolina, and Villanova.

I called all the special teams coaches and left voicemail messages over and over. But, at first, there were no return calls. After a few weeks, the coach from Villanova returned my call and said he'd let me come visit.

Villanova was the closest school on my list. It was near Philadelphia, six hours from Erie. At the athletic office, I met with the coach in charge of kickers. He was dressed head to toe in navy blue, white, and light blue, with a giant V on his shirt. I delivered my sales pitch and asked him what he'd thought of the video I'd sent before I arrived.

He told me I had a strong leg, but needed to know my statistics. I told him five out of 15 but I'm working really hard on my accuracy. Without hesitating, he told me to not transfer and that I wouldn't get any playing time at Villanova.

I walked out of his office in disbelief. I had driven six hours for nothing?

I added the coach to the list of non-believers. There had to be a school out there willing to give me a chance.

As I drove back to Erie, I stared out the window at the endless shades of green farmland dotted with silos, cows, and barns with the words "Mail Pouch Tobacco" painted on the side.

My parents told me I should stay at Gannon. "You're already the starting kicker."

They just loved me and wanted me to be safe.

When I thought about giving up, I told myself I didn't want to live with any regrets. If I didn't do this, I'd always look back and wonder, what if?

I no longer cared about playing it safe. The University of Pittsburgh was just two hours south of Erie. The closest big school. It didn't matter how many kickers were already there, this had to be it. No more what ifs.

My friend Andy Tsouris was attending summer classes at the University of Pittsburgh. We'd met in high school on a soccer all-star team. Andy had a crooked nose that accented his personality; he didn't give a shit what people thought about him. He was short and his black hair never moved. He introduced me to gyros at the Erie Greek Festival, admonishing me, "It's not *gy-ro*, it's *yee-ro!*"

I gave him a call at his apartment to ask if he wanted a visitor. In the background, I could hear sirens and honking horns.

"What's all that noise?" I asked.

"It's called the big city, stupid."

I told him I was coming down on Friday.

Just a few miles out from the city, the highway was still surrounded by trees. As I rounded the bend, I spotted tall buildings, all dwarfed by the black US Steel Tower. I had been to Pittsburgh once before, when I missed four field goals against Duquesne University, but I had blocked most of that experience out. Today, it seemed fresh, new, and full of wonder and opportunity. I recalled my only other big-city experience at the time: When I was about 12 years old, my dad had taken me to a Cleveland Browns football game. He'd gotten the cheapest seats, in the splintering red wooden bleachers behind the goalposts. This was where I'd learned creative swear words and gotten my first whiff of pot.

The Pitt campus was set in the bustling neighborhood of Oakland. People filled the sidewalks, moving among art and science museums, hospitals, towering dorms, parks, libraries, and brick apartment buildings. Andy was at work, so I embarked on a self-guided tour of the campus. I took in the beautiful architecture and walked past the centerpiece of the campus, the Cathedral of Learning, a Gothic masterpiece that boasted the distinction of being the largest educational building in the Western Hemisphere. Inside, dimly lit stone arches and ancient wooden tables tucked into mysterious nooks and hallways. It felt sacred and magical, a place where footsteps echoed down shadowy corridors and one suspected the existence of secret passageways.

I walked up to the stadium on Desota Street, aka Cardiac Hill. It was an insanely steep climb. Once inside, I asked to see the person in charge of recruiting and walk-ons. The receptionist put in a call to Larry Petroff, the recruiting coordinator, and let me know he would be out in a few minutes.

As I waited, I wandered around the lobby and halls. Displayed prominently was a glass trophy case beneath a blue-and-gold sign with the words "Pitt Football: Nine-Time National Champions." The case was filled with nine gold footballs inscribed with the dates and scores of the games. On the wall was a giant poster of the cover of a 1977 *Sports Illustrated*. The cover exclaimed, "Pitt Is It," and showed Tony Dorsett, the winner of the Heisman Trophy that year, celebrating their National Championship in the end zone alongside the Pitt mascot, the panther, with his finger signaling "number one." A replica of his Heisman Trophy was displayed on a nearby table. Another wall featured the names and photos of "Pitt Panthers in the NFL." They took up the entire wall. I pictured myself up there someday. Another wall featured pictures of seven Pitt players in the NFL Hall of Fame, including Dorsett, Dan Marino, and Mike Ditka.

A man approached. His tan khakis were a giveaway that he was a coach. An intimidating presence, he was 6-foot-3 and looked like he had played himself back in the day.

"Larry Petroff," he said as he extended his hand.

I gave my 60-second sales pitch. He didn't seem to listen.

"Here's how it works. As you know, since you are transferring, you can't play this fall. You know that, right?"

I nodded.

"So you would have to wait until February for spring ball. That's when we lift, run, and then practice outside in March. Also, we have three kickers already on scholarship. And as a walk-on, you probably won't play."

"Yes, I know," I said, but thought, *yes I will.*

"Leave Sheryl your contact information. We have a meeting for potential walk-ons in January. If you can *get through* spring ball, then you can have a spot on the team."

Our three-minute standing meeting was over.

But that was enough for me. Sign me up.

When I met with the admissions lady, she tried to burst my bubble.

"You have the grades to get into Pitt and we would accept you. However . . ."

No, no howevers.

"If you transfer to Pitt, you'll lose 12 credits. If you want *my* advice," she said, and before I could respond that I *didn't* want her advice, she concluded, "you shouldn't transfer."

I'd just pretend she never said that. Problem solved.

There would be at least three kickers ahead of me on the depth chart, but I figured that if I trained like a maniac, I could sort out my accuracy problems, and I would earn the starting spot.

My only shot was the longest shot. I applied to Pitt and got in.

• • •

Later that summer, I was playing in a bar soccer league on a team sponsored by Scully's Pub; we wore green jerseys with a shamrock on the chest. After games, we would hit the pub, which sat near a dock where a lighthouse looked out over the bay of Lake Erie and kids would park their cars and place their boom boxes on the hoods. One night, after a couple of warmups at Scully's, Andy and I headed a few doors down to Docksider's Bar, a popular watering hole that featured live music.

We'd just started our first round when Karen walked into the bar with a friend. She wore a pink flowered shirt and her usual crescent-moon smile. Her brown hair was cut short in an angled bob. She looked beautiful.

It had been three years since I'd sat with her in the basement at the high school graduation party. That was the last time we had seen or spoken with each other.

After a warm hug, I asked her what she was doing there.

"I'm home for the summer from Fordham. Edinboro was in the middle of cow pastures. I was going nuts there. So I just looked up schools in New York City and found Fordham." As she spoke, she swayed and bounced on her feet.

We chatted some more, and I found out that she had a boyfriend named Wesley.

She lifted her knee.

Karen was wearing tiny worn jean shorts with frays. While doing my best not to get caught staring at her legs, she told me she tore her ACL playing on the club lacrosse team.

"I'm sorry."

"I'm scheduled to have ACL surgery at the Cleveland Clinic next week, so I'll be around all summer," she said and poked me in the belly.

Then, with a smile that made my heart flip, she added, "We should hang out."

She grabbed a cardboard coaster from the bar and asked the bartender for a pen.

She scribbled and handed it to me. A phone number with the words "Call me, Karen" encircled in a heart.

We shared a couple of rounds of drafts, and once I was home, I couldn't sleep.

The next week, when Karen came home from her surgery in Cleveland, I brought her a teddy bear and offered to be her personal chauffeur for the remainder of the summer. One day, she showed me photos from her life at school and shared a few pictures of herself with Wesley having a great time together.

I visited her a couple of days a week. Her mother, Linda, a public school teacher, now lived in a Cape Cod on a quiet, tree-lined street near the bay. She had a beautiful sunroom that looked out over a manicured yard with a 200-year-old cherry tree. Karen and I would sit under it and talk and talk. She would laugh at all my jokes, nudge my shoulder, ask lots of questions, and always ask what I was doing each night. I felt hopeful she liked me more than just as a friend.

One evening, I asked if she wanted to get some ice cream and watch the sun set over Lake Erie.

We drove to Sarah's, a 1950s diner equipped with a jukebox and red pleather booths. We ordered two vanilla cones dipped in chocolate and walked across the street to the beach.

We found a flat spot on the sand next to a poplar tree. As the sun basked us in a warm orange glow, I asked about life in New York City and she couldn't stop beaming.

She told me how she traveled around the city every weekend via the subway with her friends and explored neighborhoods like Soho, Alphabet City, and Little Italy. Then she asked me if I liked Gannon.

"I do, but I'm transferring to Pitt. I want to play football there. I want to play in the NFL. And I figure I only get one shot in college. So why not try? I know it sounds crazy." When I had told my friends at Gannon that I was transferring to play Division I, most gave me a look of "yeah, sure you will." So I was afraid to bring it up to the person I wanted to impress the most.

"I don't think it sounds crazy at all," she said as her eyes lit up.

I thought about kissing her. It seemed like good timing. The sun had set. Everything about the moment felt romantic. But I chickened out. I thought, *too risky. Boyfriend. Too soon.*

I was getting anxious as summer's end approached, with her return to New York City and her boyfriend looming ever closer. While she was recovering from surgery, he never came to visit. I thought, *he's going to blow it.* I hoped he *would* blow it. My crush had now reached an off-the-charts level.

I kicked and lifted every day. I purchased a pocket-size, spiral-bound notebook to keep track of my progress. The sun had baked my usual practice field with the rusty goalposts until it resembled a desert with cracked dirt and stones. So I upgraded my practice facility to a new field at Mercyhurst College. They watered it every morning, and it was usually abandoned in the summer when the students had gone home.

I preplanned my training in my notebook. Along the left side of the paper, I'd written down yard measurements in increments of five from 20 yards to 60. Along the top from left to right, I'd marked "L" for left hash, "M" for middle, and "R" for right hash. A hash mark is a one-yard painted line. Two sets of hash marks run parallel to each other down the length of the field approximately 40 feet apart. If the ball is placed on a hash mark, it creates an angle for the kicker to kick the ball through the goalposts.

I would toss some blades of grass in the air to get a sense of the direction of the wind. Then I was ready to begin my marathon training session. Two kicks from the left hash 20 yards out, then two kicks from the center, then two kicks from the right hash. I would write in my results. And then I would keep going, moving back in five-yard increments until I completed my last two kicks from the right hash 60 yards away from the goalposts. Many days, my leg would get tired. But I kept going until the chart was complete.

When I was done, I would sit in the grass and leaf through the notebook looking for patterns of weakness.

In addition to accuracy, I was always trying to push the limit of my range. The NFL record at the time was 63 yards, set by Tom Dempsey of the New Orleans Saints on November 8, 1970, when I was nine months old. Dempsey was born with no fingers on his right hand and without toes on his right foot. He wore a specially designed shoe with a flattened and enlarged toe surface that resembled a sledgehammer. He kicked in that straight, head-on style like my former coach, Pat Comer. His record would stand for 43 years until Matt Prater of the Denver Broncos hit a 64-yarder in 2013.

One afternoon, my kicks were clearing the goalposts with more room to spare than usual. Fifty yards out, no problem. Move back. Fifty-five yards, no problem. Sixty yards, no problem. I decided to go for a new personal record.

When you back up, you usually need to adjust the trajectory of the kick to make the ball fly farther. In other words, you need to kick it lower. Which is why many long field goals get blocked. I placed the ball on what would have been my team's 47 yard line, making it a 63-yard attempt when you add in the 10 yards for the end zone. I took a new approach that I had been experimenting with: three steps back and one and a half over. The shortened angle seemed to be helping me with my accuracy.

The ball blasted off my foot and traveled end over end and cleared the crossbar comfortably. I had just kicked a field goal the same distance as Tom Dempsey. Granted, I didn't have the pressure of a packed NFL stadium and giant linemen trying to block the kick. I went back two more yards. Sixty-five yards. Again good. My leg felt tired. Let's try 70. I drilled the ball. It was a screaming, end-over-end line drive and nicked the crossbar as it went over. Good. My confidence grew to a new level. Nothing could stop me now. I would be the kicker at Pitt.

I gathered up my balls, tee, homemade wood-and-scrap-metal ball holder, and notebook and tossed them in my white mesh bag. In the parking lot, as I sat on the fender and took off my cleats, I felt a quick and sharp twinge of pain in my lower back. I stood by my car with my hand on my back, holding my breath. After a few seconds, the pain disappeared. I tossed my cleats into the trunk and thought, *it's probably nothing.*

• • •

A few nights before Karen and I had to leave Erie, we were in a bar engaged in our usual flirting. I started thinking that a goodnight kiss could be possible.

"Would you like to go back to the beach?" I suggested.

"Nah, let's go to Dominick's. I love their fries and ranch dressing."

Damn. Blocked.

Dominick's was a 24-hour greasy spoon in downtown Erie specializing in fried and oily grub such as the Famous Meatball Omelet and Big Italian Sandwich stuffed with ham, pepperoni, and salami. At 1:00 a.m., it was packed with drunk kids, policemen, and waitresses who looked like Flo from the 80s sitcom *Alice.*

Karen brought her A-game and requested a large order of fries with extra ranch dressing. She couldn't seem to get enough of the ranch. She made it clear that she was far more interested in her deep-fried snack than a late-night make-out session.

As I drove her back to her mom's house, I wondered if there was any chance Karen considered this a date. I parked quietly in front of her house. With my nerves riding high, I tried to keep the conversation going until it was time to walk her to the door.

"What are you doing tomorrow?" I asked.

"I don't know. What about you? Kick and lift?" Karen said with a snicker. She turned the radio up. "Joyride" by Roxette was playing. "I love this song!" She sang as her hair flew everywhere.

After she was through, I thought this was going to be the last time I saw her before I left for Pitt. I decided to go for it.

I leaned over and kissed her. The residue of fries and dressing tasted like I was making out with a sexy McDonald's Happy Meal. It lasted five seconds, until Karen pulled away. She giggled and looked down. I didn't know what to make of it. But I knew I didn't want my time with her to ever end.

For the next couple of days, I obsessively thought about Karen. While I trained and lifted, her face kept appearing in my mind. Even though my football success never seemed to matter to Karen, I thought, *if I could become an NFL kicker, maybe she would like me.*

Should I call her and tell her how I felt about her? If I did, what if I got the old *I just want to be friends* line?

As I packed my bags, I decided, screw this, I'm calling her. What did I have to lose? So I went up to my quiet place in the attic. It was mid-August and the room had taken on a humid, musty smell.

For a few days, I'd written potential openers and lines in a spiral notebook. Before dialing, I rehearsed one last time what I was going to say. I wanted to express my feelings, but not too much. I had to play it cool. I got out my notebook and began jotting down new lines. After scratching out multiple options, I finally came up with what I thought was the winning line. I dialed.

Maybe she won't answer.

"Hello," Karen said in her raspy voice.

"Hi. It's Sean," I said. "I just wanted to say goodbye one more time."

"Oh."

With my heart pounding and my voice trembling, I said, "I think we could make a great team."

Silence.

Ugh. Had I just said *make a great team* to a girl I liked?

"Yeah," she said without much feeling. "Okay."

Not exactly the resounding affirmation I was hoping for.

CHAPTER 6
FOURTH AND LONG

On the first day of classes, I grabbed my backpack and walked 15 minutes down Fifth Avenue past giant stone apartment buildings with green awnings and the Mellon Library, which looked like the Parthenon. I had rented a one-room efficiency on the fourth floor of a red brick building with another student. It was August of 1991 at the University of Pittsburgh campus. I was a fourth-year junior.

Kids scurried across the streets to the chirping sounds of the crosswalks. Buses came at me in the opposite direction in a designated bus lane. The Cathedral of Learning soared over me, making me feel small yet optimistic.

I walked into a cavernous auditorium for Geology 101 and a couple hundred students filled the room. Two giant human specimens dressed in matching white-and-blue Pitt football shirts and sweatpants sat down next to me. I said "hey" and got nothing in response. They were so large they left a seat in between them for shoulder room. It was the first time I had ever seen Division I football players this close. They looked as if they could have eaten a Gannon linebacker as a snack.

I considered introducing myself to the giants, but thought it was better to stay invisible for the moment, as I was just a walk-on, a wannabe.

In short order, I found my classes were more challenging than they'd been at Gannon, but I was focused. Around 2:00 p.m., I would get back to my apartment, drop off my backpack full of books, and then sling my ball bag over my shoulder and head out to do a solo practice. After kicking, I would go back to study by myself at the Cathedral in a room resembling Hogwarts and then get some fries with Andy.

On my first weekend on campus, the football team was playing at West Virginia University. The reality of the NCAA rule set in. I would be a spectator—a fan—for a whole season.

I wasn't able to use Pitt's facility yet, so I spent most of my training sessions that fall at Carnegie Mellon University, a private school separated from Pitt's campus by the historic Carnegie Museum of Art & Natural History buildings. The artificial turf field was open to everyone and was just a 10-minute walk from my apartment. I kicked almost every day, often 50 to 100 balls. No matter how tired my leg got, I didn't stop until I hit my goal number. I figured the *more* I kicked, the better I would get. My footballs got so worn down that the stitching came undone at the ends and the black rubber bladder peeked out. I still used a notebook to record how many kicks I'd made and from which distance, as if kicking footballs were some sort of math problem to be solved.

I trained the same way in the student weight room. I planned out what I would do, how much I would lift, and no matter how tired my body felt, I didn't stop. And I expanded my training beyond kicking and lifting. I tested my body to see how much abuse it could take. I did wind sprints and ran up and down the hills and steps of Pittsburgh's neighborhoods like I was Rocky Balboa training to fight Apollo Creed.

When you kick a football, you repeat the same motion every time. It creates amazing torque in your lower back and hips. I started to have back pain and literal pain in my ass, along with shooting pains down the sides of my leg. But because of my intense focus, kicking less wasn't something I'd ever consider.

One day, I told Andy about my back pain.

"Dude, you should go to a chiropractor. My dad is going to one in Erie and he said his back has never felt better."

I'd seen signs on the street with pictures of spines in their logos, but I'd never given it a thought.

I found one three blocks from my apartment. After an initial examination and X-rays, the chiropractor showed me the images and explained the imbalances and compressions he'd found in my spine. There was also a crack in one of my vertebrae. I thought pain and injury were just part of the process. His suggested treatment was to come in once a week. The doctor worked out a cash deal with me for $20 a visit. My dad usually sent me $25 a week in cash, so I still had $5 left over for quarter drafts. To make some extra money, I worked the desk at the cafeteria on the first floor of my dorm and let my friends in for free. In exchange, they bought me beers or paid my party admission.

The treatments seemed to give me some immediate relief, but with the heavy training, it was a wash at best. I began to accept the possibility that I would always have to play through pain.

At last, February came, and I was finally allowed to walk on. The road ahead of me couldn't have been any clearer: I had just one season of eligibility left. I had one chance to prove myself. This was it. It was fight my way to a starting spot or bust.

To make the team, walk-ons had to survive the grueling winter workouts. It was about attrition. They wanted to see how committed you were. If you could get through 10 weeks and were still around at the end in mid-April, you were on the team and would receive your own locker and official gear.

The best most walk-ons hoped for was a spot on the scout team. Before every game, they helped prepare the starters by learning and replicating the next opponent's offense, defense, and special teams. Other responsibilities were holding blocking dummies, cheerleading, and keeping the bench warm for the starters. Walk-ons suited up for home games only, unless by some miracle they got playing time and got to travel with the team for road games.

Spring ball had two main components: 5:30 a.m. workouts in the indoor facility, which might include running in and out of cones, sprints, agility or jumping drills, etc., and then afternoons in the weight room. We started with 25 walk-ons. Most fizzled in the first few days, deciding it wasn't worth puking their guts out before dawn each day and being barked at, especially without a scholarship. It was easy to doubt one's decision and slip back into the leisurely life of going to classes, playing video games, and sleeping in until noon.

Not me. My determination was sky-high. Getting up early in the morning and lifting felt easy for me. It had been almost two years since I played for Gannon, so I'd been chomping at the bit to prove myself. I was hungry.

Every weekday at 5:00 a.m. in the pitch black and bitter cold, with snow falling, I crawled out of bed and headed up Cardiac Hill and ran the drills while my roommates slept off their quarter drafts from the night before.

Since I wasn't part of the team yet, I had to come up with my own gear. The "real" players had blue-and-white tops with matching bottoms and the latest footwear. The walk-ons? We looked like we came from the Land of Misfit Toys. We wanted so badly to fit in, we bought gear that we thought *looked* like that of the current players. Most of us did not resemble Division I athletes; some of us were short, some stalky or lanky, and some slow, but in our heads and hearts, we wanted desperately to be part of something and so we kept at it.

Aside from my intermittent back pain, I was in the best shape of my life. At Gannon, I was a lanky 183 pounds. I was now 195 and most of it was lean muscle.

I wanted to impress my teammates that I wasn't just an ordinary walk-on or an ordinary kicker. Kickers fight a stigma of not being considered *real players*, as they don't block, tackle, or get tackled. I didn't want to be that kind of kicker.

For walk-ons, the margin of error was slim. Any missed session or minor violation of the rules, and you could be cut in a second. We were terrified of fucking up.

The first few days of workouts were uneventful. I handled the running exercises with ease. Puking from a hard workout was considered normal, but I fought hard and managed to keep it in as a couple dozen players tossed their breakfast into rubber commercial garbage cans next to me.

But then I ran into a little bad luck—literally.

It was 5:30 in the morning. I was wearing the bright yellow cut-off Kmart sweatpants that Santa Claus had just given me, trying to blend in as we began our warmup run around the field at the indoor facility, the Cost Center. As we approached a corner, I got caught in a mass of players.

I did my best to stay outside the cone, aware that a player who went inside the cone would be punished, but I got pushed to the inside and missed the cone. I tried to jog behind another player and use his body as a shield, hoping no one had noticed. But someone had.

I heard a deep, loud southern drawl. "Hey! You in the yellow britches! You miss the cone one more time and you're gone."

It was Amos Jones. *My fucking luck!* Jones was the special teams coach, in charge of the kickers. Any of the other 20-some coaches might have been all right, but he was the coach I wanted most to impress.

At 32, Amos was just 10 years removed from playing and coaching for the most famous of college coaches, the legendary Paul "Bear" Bryant, who earned the moniker for agreeing to wrestle a captive bear at a carnival when he was just 13 years old. The longtime University of Alabama coach held the record for most wins as a head coach in collegiate football. His power was such that any alumnus who'd played for the Bear was guaranteed a full ride to the University of Alabama for their kids. As a protégé of Bryant's, Amos was self-assured with a swagger and a brash delivery. He was our only coach from the South, and at first, a lot of players saw him as a fish out of water. Like me, most of the players were northern boys from the farm towns, manufacturing centers, and steel cities of Pennsylvania and Ohio. No one quite knew what to make of Amos.

He wasn't the usual coach, who liked to yell robotically. He was a badass Andy Griffith, delivering unexpected one-liners that could knock you flat.

One day during a player meeting, a kicker was babbling on and on about how he could improve his technique. Amos watched him quietly, and then interrupted, "You're as windy as a sack full of farts."

If you were lazy, you didn't rate high in Amos's book. If you were a hard worker with a great attitude, you were in. It was that simple. Amos was the type of coach who liked to take average players who worked hard and turn them into stars. To him, attitude and work ethic were everything; if you had those, he'd help you get better.

When March came, it was time to go outside and actually practice playing football. Time to bring out the balls. Time to kick and fight for a position.

The odds could not have been stacked higher against me, since Pitt already had four kickers on the team, three of them on scholarship. On day one, I was named fifth-string kicker on the depth chart. I had just five months to pass four kickers, and none of the top four seemed happy that I'd shown up out of nowhere to try to take their jobs.

The third-string kicker was Tommy Donatelli, a local legend from Pittsburgh who'd made one of the longest kicks in Pennsylvania high school history. The second-string kicker was Ed Frazier, who in a legendary 1989 Pitt game had kicked a 42-yard field goal to tie the game on the last play against rival West Virginia. The current starter was Steve Kelly, who strode around like he was the man. He'd been the starter the past two years. But my biggest threat was my mind.

On the first day of practice, Amos told us to line up and practice kickoffs.

In college football, the ball is placed on the 35 yard line and you try to kick it as far and as high as possible. A good kick stays in the air for at least four seconds and reaches the goal line—65 yards away. The amount of time the ball is in the air is called hang time. Good hang time allows the coverage team to get downfield and make a tackle deep in the opponent's zone. Coaches want the ball to go into the end zone for strategic and safety reasons. If the player catches the ball in the end zone, he can elect to set his knee on the ground, and the play is dead. A touchback. No one gets hurt, and the team starts the ball from the 20 yard line. Kickoffs have the highest rates of injury of any play; many football experts call it the most dangerous play in the game. Fast and strong players sprint toward each other, then collide violently, sometimes causing injury, including concussions—and, in rare instances, paralysis.

Amos pulled out his stopwatch. We took our turns, one at a time. There couldn't have been an easier way to show who had the strongest leg.

The trick to kicking off is trying not to over-kick it—not trying too hard. If I tried to crush it, the ball could flub down the field like a kite crashing down in the wind.

Since I was last on the depth chart, I had to wait my turn for the four kickers who were already on the team. I didn't notice how they performed.

I was too busy visualizing my kicks landing in the end zone. I was concerned that my leg would start shaking or my heart would start racing. But it didn't. I felt more excited than nervous. It was now or never. There was no "maybe next year will be it." No more schools to transfer to. Pitt was it.

As it neared my turn, I grabbed a ball and started squeezing it.

"Conley, you're up," Amos shouted.

I placed the ball on the red tee and adjusted it to the precise angle, slightly tilted back and to the right. I glanced down at the ball to double check that it was set right. I jogged 10 yards back, turned around to face the ball, and moved a few yards over to the left. I fixed my eyes on the ball then looked 65 yards away at the end zone. A lone kick returner wearing a #26 jersey stood on the goal line. I visualized kicking the ball so far that he would have to back up to catch it.

I approached at a slow jog and struck the ball with what felt like the right amount of power. Not too hard, not too soft. Without even looking up yet, I knew the ball was going deep. I completed my follow-through and looked up. #26 looked up at the sky and walked slowly backward until he caught the ball about seven yards deep in the end zone, just a few steps in front of the goalposts.

My next three kicks also went beyond the goal line into the end zone. I counted in my head as the balls soared high and deep, floating end over end toward the end zone, *one, two, three, four* . . . My last one went beyond the *back* line of the end zone. After the last kick, I heard a southern drawl from behind me: "I saw that, son," Amos said.

I had kicked higher and farther than all the other kickers. I could taste being on the team.

As camp went on, field goals were a different story. On one out of every five kicks or so, my ball would rotate sideways in the air. The other kickers, with the exception of Eddie, would yell out, "Helicopter," and laugh, enjoying my failure. I still couldn't figure out what was causing the balls to fly like that. I tried to block out their jabs.

A couple nights before our annual Blue-Gold Game, which marked the end of spring camp, I was in Peter's Pub near campus. Sitting at the corner of the bar was Dan Marino, the top NFL quarterback at the time and a legend at Pitt from 1979 to 1982. We shared a beer and he imparted some great advice for being an NFL kicker. He asked me if I was any good. I responded, "Yeah, I'm pretty good." He grabbed me by the shirt and pulled me closer to him and said: "Pretty good? The answer is, *I'm the best f-ing kicker ever!*"

In the scrimmage amongst teammates, using added inspiration from Dan, I tried to show the coaches I was the best f-ing kicker ever. I made all of my field goal attempts. It was my last chance to prove myself until summer training camp. Amos approached me and asked me back to his office.

As we walked along the hard artificial turf, the stadium emptied out.

I was no longer feeling intimidated by Amos.

"Have a seat, son. You've had one helluva spring season, don't you think?" Then, with his eyebrows raised, he said, "Congratulations. You've earned a spot on the team. I'm going to tell the equipment managers to give you your own locker."

I wanted to throw my fist into the air.

"Son, I don't care if you've been playing four years or four days. I'm going to start the best guy. I'm jumping you up to number three on the depth chart for field goals. And for kickoffs, I'm putting you number one."

Number one.

I stayed cool, trying to contain my enthusiasm.

"You remind me of a kicker I had down in Tuscaloosa, Alabama. You have a cannon for a leg, and your head is on straight, unlike some of those bozo kickers I see out there these days. But sometimes when you kick a field goal," he added, "the ball flies in the air like a doggone helicopter."

He grabbed his laser pointer and popped in a video of one of our practices with a close-up of me kicking. We watched the kicks that I hit clean and the ones with the helicopter ball. "See, look there, son," he said. "Your foot is hitting the ball too high. You're missing the sweet spot. And look what your foot is doing when you hit it right. You clean this up, and you could be an All-American."

Amos understood my soccer-style approach.

"You need to pay more attention to your mechanics. Sometimes you just try to crush the ball into outer space. What good is it if your balls land on Mars when they are supposed to land on the moon?"

The man had a point.

I sat and listened. He wanted me to be his guy. He believed in me. And now I didn't want to let him down. I wanted to lace up my cleats and sprint into the stadium and start kicking.

"One other thing," Amos said. "I see some of the other kickers trying to get in your head. Don't let them. Each one of them was recruited and given a scholarship and probably promised they would be the starter. They're not happy about you showing up out of thin air trying to take their job. One of them kisses more ass than a toilet seat. That's not how you win a job with me. Keep working hard and don't listen to any bullshit they toss at you."

I nodded. From then on, I enjoyed their trash talk as it just motivated me more.

He tossed the VCR remote onto my lap. "I've got to go. I have a coaches' meeting."

He stopped at the door. "You know," he said, "you won't be successful if you just focus on what you do wrong."

He paused.

"When Coach Bryant walked into the auditorium after a game, he showed the team film from the previous game. He hardly ever showed the players their mistakes. He mostly showed them plays that they were successful in."

"Really?" I said.

"Give most of your attention to your good kicks." And off he went.

In that moment, something changed. I would focus more on my successes and give less attention to my failures.

I sat in his office for a couple of hours watching videos and came back the next day. I studied the position of my plant foot. The remote control was glued to my hand. I went over and over the tapes. I could see the difference when I hit it right and wrong. And then, taking Amos's advice, I watched some of the good kicks again and again until the right way to kick was cemented in my mind. Going forward, I replayed in my mind scenes of success and positivity. Brushing my teeth, lying in bed at night, on the field, the film clip in my mind showed the ball soaring beautifully through the posts.

I was excited to be named the starter for kickoffs. But I wanted to be number one for field goals as well. I scarcely paused to celebrate the victory because I was too focused on training and improving—on my perfectionist quest.

There was always time to celebrate with Andy, though. On Saturday night, Andy was already out and I told him I'd meet him around 11:00. I invited over a girl, Liz, whom I was seeing for the third time. Liz was great, but if I was honest with myself, I was still obsessed with Karen. Liz, who lived down the hall, was sweet, sleek, and pretty, with dark hair, and always dressed in sharp black skirts. In fact, she dressed like Karen and even looked like Karen. We were sharing a couple of Milwaukee's Best on my bed, listening to Prince and Terence Trent D'Arby on Andy's four-foot-tall mega stereo with concert-size speakers, when my phone rang.

"Hello?"

"Hey, I'm so excited I got you," said a very familiar voice.

It had been eight months since I'd talked to Karen on the phone, when she'd shot down my "we'd make a great team" line.

But with Liz sitting a few feet away on the bed listening to my every word, I curbed my enthusiasm.

"I called your mom in Erie to get your number. I'm so glad I tracked you down," Karen exclaimed.

"That's great," I said.

"Is there someone in the room with you?" she asked.

"Yes," I said. I could feel Liz's eyes burning the back of my head.

"Is it a girl?" Karen asked.

"Umm. Sort of," I said.

"She's sort of a girl?" Karen giggled.

Awkward silence.

"I'm sorry. It's okay. Bad timing. I'll call you later," Karen said.

Then we hung up.

"Who was that?" Liz asked.

"Um, just a friend from high school."

"What's her name?"

"Let's get out of here and go meet our friends."

Liz wasn't about to let me dodge the subject that easily. It became clear we wouldn't be dating much longer, as the interrogation continued throughout the night, but I didn't care. I was dreaming of seeing Karen again. I was surprised that she seemed concerned that I was with a girl. *Maybe*, I thought, *she actually likes me.*

CHAPTER 7
UNDERDOG

scarfed down three bowls of Cap'n Crunch, a handful of horse-size amino acid pills, and a protein shake and then set out for Cardiac Hill. That morning, I felt like I was gliding instead of struggling on what was usually a strenuous walk.

I'd decided to stay in Pittsburgh over the summer to train and take two classes to make up for the credits I'd lost when I transferred.

I threw the bag over my shoulder and headed out. It was 9:00 a.m. and the sun was beginning to warm the turf. I gazed at the empty seats and imagined what it might feel like playing in front of a packed stadium. I chanted to myself, *Stay focused. Train as hard and as much as possible. Don't let up. Three months to get ready.*

The summer of 1992 became the summer of training insanity.

"Cons!"

I turned to find John Bruner and Lou Casanova, both fellow walk-ons. Lou was a snapper for field goals and extra points; John was a wide receiver. At the end of spring ball, John had offered to hold field goals for me during the summer.

Remembering the tips and drills Amos had given me for eliminating my "helicopter ball," I focused on hitting the sweet spot with my foot angled in the precise position. The ball's sweet spot is tiny. Missing it by less than a centimeter can cause the ball to go off course or travel through the air like a wounded duck.

I began to look at my craft more as an art than a competition to be the best, and it made an enormous difference. Visualize. Repetition. Sweet spot. Strike it. Not too hard, not too soft. Without even looking up, I knew my kicks were good when I hit the ball.

In just a few days, the helicopter ball disappeared and my kicks were sailing end over end. My field goals became laser-sharp. When I missed a kick, I knew exactly why I'd missed. I started to aim for the goalposts every once in a while just to test my accuracy. I was no longer thinking when I kicked. I was just feeling.

This was an unconventional strategy for me. I had trained my mind to be busy at all times. Now, if I could turn down the ranting in my head, I could accomplish more by trusting my body's intuitive powers.

To work on my height—or, in football terms, "trajectory" or "lift"— I'd line up as close as I could to the goalposts and try to clear them. After some practice, I could get within five yards and clear the 10-foot crossbar.

"I think you're good, Cons. My arms are getting tired," Lou said.

"Five more," I said.

"Let's go lift now. You're done," John said.

I wanted to keep going.

John stood up and handed me the ball. "You don't have to crush it. Your perfectionism is fucking with your head. Just hit it nice and easy."

John would be by my side all summer. Holding hundreds of balls. Always reminding me to just be steady. Consistent.

The weight room was like a Gold's Gym on, well . . . steroids. Every size dumbbell and barbell as far as the eye could see. The walls were decorated with endless painted wooden plaques showing off every bowl game Pitt had ever played in: Rose Bowl, Gator Bowl, Sugar Bowl, Fiesta Bowl, Sun Bowl, and more. The stereo was jamming "Baby Got Back" by Sir Mix-a-Lot. A pink substance was foaming in a soda fountain. Unlimited protein drinks to pack on muscle.

As we walked in, the strength coach handed us our detailed workout for the day. Squats, deadlifts, bench press, dumbbell curls.

"Get started, guys."

A handful of scholarship guys were lifting on the other side of the room. Each one was bigger than the next, including the two giants from Geology 101.

This became my daily routine. Each morning during the summer until camp began in mid-August: kick and lift. It was like a mantra. Kick and lift. Kick and lift. I rarely took a day off to rest. I walked up to the Pitt training facility around 8:00 every morning and left around noon. There, I would lift, then stretch, then kick, then maybe lift again, then run some sprints.

After one more calorie-packed cup of protein shake so I didn't have to go out for lunch, I headed back down to my favorite spot on campus: the Cathedral lawn. The green oasis was alive with summer-schoolers. Girls were sunning, reading books. Boys tossed Frisbees. I opened my textbooks and plugged in my Discman and got lost in my football fantasy world. My piece of crap apartment didn't have air-conditioning so there was no incentive to go back. Plus, I felt collegiate studying outside of the Cathedral. Looking up at the clouds, I played Tom Petty's "Runnin' Down a Dream" on repeat until I fell asleep.

The season couldn't start soon enough.

• • •

The dormitory was silent with the exception of the crickets. It was nine or ten o'clock at night. I sat alone in my sparse cinder-block dorm room. My roommate, one of the backup quarterbacks, was in a meeting in another building with the offense. While they were meeting, my dormitory had a population slightly greater than that of the North Pole: two. One kicker and one long snapper.

We were in Johnstown, Pennsylvania, about an hour east of Pittsburgh in the Laurel Highland Mountains. This was our home for the three-week camp; they'd put us out here to keep us from the distractions of campus and the city.

"Hey kicker, what's up?" It was Lou.

"Hey snapper," I said.

Lou took a seat on the bed across from me. He smiled brighter than the gold chain around his neck.

"Dude, why are you looking at me like that?" I asked.

"Amos just told me I'm the starting long snapper for all field goals and punts."

"Are you serious? Congratulations, man."

A long snapper is the guy who hikes the ball for punts and field goals—a craft that's much harder than it looks. In a bent-over position, the long snapper hikes the ball between his legs at a blazing speed, making it travel in a tight spiral with pinpoint accuracy. The best ones can zip the ball at over 50 miles an hour. Long snappers have three jobs in one: hiking the ball for extra points, field goals, and punts. It's a thankless, glory-less job. They get noticed only when they snap the ball over the holder's or punter's head.

"I'm pulling for you," Lou said. "How great would it be if two walk-ons were the starting kicker and snapper?"

"The other kickers are pretty good." I paused. "But I think I'm better."

"It's not even close," Lou said.

Despite his assurances, I didn't think Coach Hackett wanted me to win the job. The other kickers had proven themselves in real games. I was a risky pick.

"Amos loves you," Lou said. "I don't think that Amos gives a shit that you're a walk-on. He's an outsider here too."

At 10:00 p.m., it was lights out. The kicking battle would resume in the morning.

• • •

On the path through the woods to the practice field, a sign taped to a giant oak tree read "Twenty-Four Days Until Kent State."

The grass was yellow. It had been weeks since the field had seen rain. The sunbaked practice field was hard and difficult for cleats to grip. Each practice was the same: first Steve, then Eddie, and then me. I made almost every kick and my balls went higher and farther, and yet, I stayed stuck at third on the depth chart. Amos kept telling me when he caught me alone, "Keep doing what you're doing, son."

I tried not to *root* for the other kickers to miss. Remembering what Amos told me. Just focus on what I need to. Nice and easy. My competition was just my mind. I could feel them still hoping I would fall apart, hoping I was a flash in the pan.

The days seemed the same too: 85 steamy degrees, sunny, muggy, no air-conditioning, three practices a day, meals, meetings, lights out, and repeat.

One morning, the sign read "Just Ten Days Until Kent State." When I made it to the field, the other kickers, punters, and snappers were adjusting their pads and equipment. Lou approached me slyly and pulled me to the side.

"Hey, kicker, it's just you and Eddie now."

"What are you talking about?" I asked.

"Steve has appendicitis. He's going to be out for at least three weeks."

Illness and injuries were part of the cold reality of camp. No one seemed concerned. I wasn't. I felt confident I would win the job in the end. But it helped clear my path. I was ready to show Coach Hackett and Amos that beyond any doubt, I was the best option.

For the final two days of camp, Amos had me and Eddie alternating kicks. Eddie first, me second. Even though we were competing against each other, Eddie and I developed a friendly rapport. Unlike him, I had no track record of playing under pressure at the Division I level, just my history of game-day futility in Division III; I'd have to perform convincingly to make my case to be the starter. Eddie was part of Pitt lore with his game-tying field goal against West Virginia two years earlier.

But my kicks went farther and higher.

Amos stood next to Coach Hackett. Amos would murmur something and gesture after I kicked, and Coach Hackett, wearing tinted prescription aviators, would just stand motionless with his arms crossed.

"Everyone bring it in," Coach Hackett yelled through the microphone to the whole team. The hundred or so players circled around him and took a knee while the other coaches and staff stood behind us.

"Conley and Frazier are going to alternate field goals now in a live setting."

Shit just got real.

"Make as much noise as possible while they kick," he said to the team. "Do whatever you can to distract them."

"Frazier, you go first. Five 40-yard field goals."

As Eddie lined up, guys jumped up and down and told "your mama" jokes and hooped and hollered. He made his first three kicks, but the last two sailed wide right. As he walked back, he looked at me and said, "Good luck," and I slapped his hand.

"Men, get even louder, taunt him," Coach Hackett yelled.

The noise only made me more excited. I heard someone say, "You're gonna shank it kicker." And "Hey kicker, you suck!"

I made all five kicks.

I couldn't help glancing over at Amos standing next to Coach Hackett. Amos had his arms out, palms turned up to the sky, as if he were asking, *Does that convince you?*

Amos walked over to Eddie and me and guided us over by an old tree on the sidelines.

"Good job men," he said. "We have no starting kicker. The starter will be decided on game day before kickoff."

• • •

By the end of Pitt's preseason practice, the coaches had named the starters for every position except one. Kicker.

Game day arrived. I had hoped I'd have the starting kicker position all sewn up by the end of preseason so I could relax before the first game. But that would have been too easy. The head coach had his reservations about me: no game experience, no scholarship, and an unproven walk-on. He was leaning toward Eddie. Eddie had history.

I trotted out for the first-game warmups for one last battle to decide the starting kicker, still and always proving myself.

Eddie and I took turns kicking. Amos stood watching from the sideline, stone-faced. Just as I had at practice all week, I outkicked Eddie.

Still, 30 minutes from kickoff and there seemed to be no decision. I looked up to see my parents finding their seats in the stands. The contest for starter took on a new urgency. I made the final two practice kicks, both from 50 yards out.

"That's it men, head on in," Amos called. He put his arm around me on my way to the locker room and led me to the corner of the goal line.

"Son, you're our starting kicker."

My heart surged. I kept my game face on because showing the incredible emotion that was churning my gut right at that moment would have been a violation of the unwritten football macho rules.

"Those other kickers can't even hold your doggone jockstrap. I've had you pegged as the starter since the first time I saw you kick back in March. I believe in you." He slapped me on my helmet. "Go get ready."

As I headed back to my locker, I tried to stay calm. I made it. But I was about to be in the spotlight. It could end in a flash. Or in this case, a missed kick. I'd played in front of hundreds at Gannon. In a few minutes, it would be tens of thousands.

Eddie approached me where I sat on the bench and extended his hand. "You deserve it. Good luck tonight."

When the game began, yellow pompoms moved in unison in the student section to the rhythm of the Pitt fight song. The sun began to fall behind the surrounding buildings. It was a warm fall evening, and the colossal stadium lights set the field ablaze.

I wore the same uniform as everyone else, but I was not a part of the aggression, smashing helmets, speed, and explosive plays. I hung out far off to the side and out of the chaos, by a practice kicking net. My only company was the punter. As a kicker, you become quiet. You go within yourself, visualizing every detail of successful kicks from different angles on the field. You try to deflect thoughts of missing a field goal on the last play of the game and being the infamous "goat" or "choker." You get one shot when you're finally called, so your mind, your leg, and your whole body need to be preprogrammed for success.

Players streamed into and out of the game, looking exhausted, wrapped in arm pads, knuckle tape, and knee braces. Meanwhile, I waited. I kept my nerves under control, remembered to breathe, visualized the perfect post-splitting kick, and waited some more. It's one big long wait for that momentary, fleeting chance to prove to myself that I am a legitimate member of the team.

At the end of the first quarter, we drove to the Kent State 29 yard line. Quarterback Alex Van Pelt dropped back to pass, and the Kent State rush collapsed the pocket. Just before he was hit, Van Pelt tossed off a high drifting pass to the legendary Pitt running back Curtis Martin. Martin jumped up in the slice of air between two defenders and improbably plucked the ball out of its arc, tumbling to the ground three yards into the end zone. Over the roar of the crowd, I could hear Coach Jones yelling, "Extra point team!" The wait was over.

My parents only realized I was the starter as they spotted my jersey number trotting onto the field to cluster with the team at the 10 yard line. For kickers, sometimes it's the easiest kicks that can be the most stressful. Just an extra point. I was never supposed to miss one of these. I lined my body up and gazed up at the goalposts. I reminded myself not to rush. Breathe. I nodded to my holder that I was ready.

The kick sailed easy and true, and I had my first Division I football point. I could do this. I just needed to kick all of them the same way.

By the time the special teams huddled at the 30 for the kickoff, I was as amped as any player that had made a sack or touchdown. In the huddle, I told the team where I would be kicking it. "Deep kick right. Deep kick right. Ready . . . break!" I set the ball on my red tee, counted off the players on either side of me, signaled for the kick, and jogged toward the ball. I blasted it into the stratosphere. The Kent State kick returner caught it deep in his own end zone, taking a knee without even thinking about running it out.

We were leading 48–10 when we stalled on the Kent State 14 yard line. Amos called in the field goal team. Having booted the point afters and kickoffs, I was warmed and ready, but I had a moment of unpleasant déjà vu. The setup was eerily familiar to my first college kick at Gannon three years earlier. It was 31 yards out and placed on the far right hash mark. For right-legged kickers, this is a nightmare kick. It's too close, at the wrong angle, and it looks simple from anywhere else in the stadium so everyone watching thinks it's an easy three.

My leg began to shake and I could hear my heart pounding. I simply could not let this kick get in my head or I would have a helluva time getting it out. I nodded to my holder, and he held up his hand to give the long snapper the green light. I took my few steps, and immediately realized damn, I hadn't squared my hips correctly. As the ball sailed, it was clear that I had the distance. From where I was standing, though, it looked like the ball went right over top of the near upright. The ball has to clearly go between the posts for the goal to be good. I stared at the zebras on either side of the goalposts as they slowly watched the ball, then even more slowly looked to each and exchanged a subtle nod. They raised their arms in unison.

My first Division I field goal. Three points, in the books. *Exhale.*

It was a great start to the season, as we inked a 51–10 win. I showered and dressed as quickly as I could to get out and see my parents before they headed home.

My mom told me she cried when I came out for the first extra point. My dad, on the other hand, wasn't about to lavish praise on me. He just smiled, clapped me on the shoulder, and slid me some cash in his parting handshake.

I didn't tell them what I already knew: There was no guarantee I'd be the starter all season. Kickers win their role kick by kick, and you're only as good as your last one. If I wanted to be at the front of the pack, if I wanted to keep Eddie on the bench, I was going to have to be on the mark for more than one game. And I discovered how hard that could be the very next week.

CHAPTER 8
HAIL MARY

Our next game, we got spanked, 44–6 by West Virginia. The game was known as the "backyard brawl" because WVU and Pitt were a mere 90 minutes apart.

After we scored our lone touchdown, I missed an extra point. Wide right. Shank. The ball careened off the cement wall with a thud. I stared at the goalposts for a moment in disbelief. A West Virginia player shouted an obscenity at me as he ran past.

It should have been a gimme. It was a chip shot from straight on that I normally could have made with my left foot.

I jogged off the field with my eyes down, as if I could stop Coach Hackett from demoting me if I didn't make eye contact. I was still the starter after the game, but I was on thin ice.

I talked to my dad almost every day. I told him if I missed my next kick, I would probably get benched. He reminded me to just relax.

Our third game was against Rutgers, at Rutgers Stadium in Piscataway, New Jersey. It was the Thursday Night Game of the Week on ESPN, which ramped up the pressure by about a factor of a thousand. The sprinklers had run too long and the field was a sloppy mud bowl for pregame warmups. It was a messy scene; all the kickers were slipping, sliding, and falling. By game time, our uniforms were filthy, making us look like "real players." It was ugly and, for me, about to get uglier.

My nerves were a jangled mess by the start of the game. I asked the equipment manager to dig me up some cleats with bigger spikes on them, so that I could use one on my plant foot.

Finally, late in the second quarter, we made progress on a drive toward the Rutgers end zone. I started kicking into the net, trying hard to think good thoughts. I needed to forget about the possibility of missing a kick on national television with my friends and family watching. Instead, I visualized myself making kick after kick on the rocky field a few blocks from my house.

Rutgers Stadium had ridiculously narrow sidelines, which meant the fans in the first rows of the stands were right on top of you. As I warmed up, drunk Rutgers college students treated me to a barrage of curses that would have been the pride of a teamster. I started to think that maybe the college had an English major with a focus on creative swearing. I blocked out the noise.

On a third-and-8, we were stopped five yards short. Amos yelled out, "Field goal team," and my stomach knotted.

A 42-yard attempt. "You have to make this," I thought to myself. Then my holder counted off our guys and found that we were one short. The ensuing confusion cost us a five-yard, delay-of-game penalty. That 42-yarder just became a 47-yarder.

I stepped into the kick and the mud monster of a field grabbed ahold of my plant foot, gluing it off center as my kicking leg tried to compensate. I watched helplessly as the ball went careening in a helicopter spin toward the exit tunnel at the corner of the end zone. Now it was my turn to spew swear words in the echo chamber of my head.

Two misses in a row. Two.

Missing a kick is a 10 times more painful feeling than the joy of making one. It's not like in golf, where a golfer can get another shot. Your last kick could really be your last.

I had no desire to let Amos down. I knew he had put himself out there to convince Coach Hackett that I was the right choice for starter. Now I had disappointed both of them, not once, but twice.

Amos met me on the sidelines. He did what he always did, played the booster.

"That kick is history, just get ready to make the next one." Then, "I believe in you." His dark brown eyes convinced me.

Those last four words hit home in a big way.

A minute later, Coach Hackett called Amos over and they had a tense exchange. I could tell that I was the subject, and it didn't look like I was getting a great big vote of confidence from my head coach.

It was now the third quarter and we were trailing 7–0. On the field, the Rutgers defensive line stuffed our fullback over tackle and it was fourth down. Amos yelled, "Field goal team."

It was all I needed—one more chance. The kick was a 44-yarder. I stood waiting for the snap, emptying my mind. I just had to trust myself and let the simple act of kicking a kick I'd made a hundred times before happen. Before I even realized it, the kick was up and away. It had the distance, and I didn't even need to see the referees raise their arms because it could not have been closer to the middle. I felt like I'd just shrugged a monkey off my back.

I jogged off the field, feeling 400 pounds lighter. The first person I came to was Coach Hackett, wearing his brown headset and holding his laminated play card with his arms raised in the air. He gave me a nod. "Way to bounce back Conley."

We lost the game 21–16, and I couldn't help feeling conflicted. I was disappointed in the loss, but incredibly relieved that I was still the starter.

It was bizarre to feel good about my performance—to feel like I'd gone through a trial by fire and come out the other side more confident and secure—while sharing a locker room with a hundred some-odd guys who were all trying not to go down the black hole of despair in a bleak losing season. It's the kicker's paradox. You could be on an undefeated team beating the crap out of every opponent, but if you made fewer than every three out of four tries, the coach would be calling for the next man up.

I'd come through the storm, the worst thing that was going to happen to me on a Division I field. Sitting on the chartered plane, I mulled things over. What if I missed the next one?

"Stop," I told myself. "You just made the most pressure-packed kick of your career." My job had been on the line. Everything I had worked to achieve would have vanished if I'd missed that kick. But I'd made it. All I had to do was *not* think about missing. As I looked out the porthole window into the pitch-black sky, I imagined myself making every single kick for the rest of the season. It seemed perfectly realistic.

Outside of practice and off the field, I continued to unwind with Andy. Like any good dorm roommate and wingman, he was always up for a trip to 7-Eleven to restock our bachelor pantry with Mountain Dew and Slim Jims. One Thursday night, making our way back to the dorm for an evening of ignoring homework, I took a peek through the window of my favorite bar, C. J. Barney's. I did a double take.

"What the . . . ?"

Inside was the most beautiful brunette waitress, carrying a pitcher of beer and a big plate of wings.

Karen.

Our eyes met and she flashed me that thousand-watt smile that was a bullet through my heart. Andy and I waltzed in and I hugged her, lifting her off the ground.

"What are you doing here?"

She laughed. "Well, I graduated from Fordham and there were no jobs in the city, so I applied back here for my master's." Somebody signaled her at a table and she grabbed my arm. "Listen, I have to take care of those guys. Don't leave," she said with a flirty wink. *She must have a boyfriend,* I thought, otherwise she would have reached out.

Andy and I sat at the bar, ordered beers, and tried to pretend things were normal and that I hadn't just stumbled across the love of my life on some random Thursday night in Pittsburgh.

"Dude, play it cool. Stop staring at her like a panting dog. Why don't you just ask her out?"

"I need a couple more beers in me first."

"How about this," Andy suggested. "Let's see if she likes you. You just act casual, don't look at her. If I see her looking at you, I'll say 'Ford Fairlane.'"

The Adventures of Ford Fairlane was a cheesy movie from 1990 starring Andrew Dice Clay that Andy and I watched almost every day in our dirty dorm room. It was also the name of my grandparents' 1970 forest-green car that was still in operation and that they let me borrow whenever I was in Erie.

I sat looking at the TV, sipping on my beer.

"Ford Fairlane!"

I turned my head so quick I pulled a muscle in my neck. Karen had her back to me, waiting on a couple.

"Ha-ha, you fucking idiot. You just got whiplash," Andy said as he messed with me.

Andy and I stayed for a couple of hours, and I talked to her as much as I could in the moments when she wasn't serving the other customers. I finally mustered the nerve to ask, "Are you still dating Wesley?"

"Nope. We broke up." She tilted her head and bit down on her lower lip. "Maybe I'll see you around?"

"Do you want to hang out next Wednesday night?"

She pulled her order notebook and a pen out of her apron, smooth as a magician. "Here's the number at my apartment. I live down on McKee Place."

A large older man approached.

"Get back to work, Karen!"

"I gotta go," she said. "Call me."

Suddenly, the world was there for the taking. I seemed a few kicks shy of the NFL, and one date away from having the relationship I'd dreamed about for the better part of five years.

When I called her the next day, she asked, "Are you ready for The Big Date?" So, this *was* a date.

With no more than chump change to my name, the pressure was on. My father sent me $25 cash each week in an envelope that showed up in my dorm mailroom without my mother's knowledge. My mom was in charge of the checkbook and tight with the dough. She thought any extra money I had would be used on beer. She was right.

The cash made a huge difference, but it wouldn't go far if I had to pay for someone else. I wanted to take Karen somewhere away from campus, where it would be quiet. I came up with Max & Erma's, similar in style to a TGIFriday's. I considered this "big time." It was in Shadyside, a quiet yuppified neighborhood a 20-minute walk from campus.

In my dorm room, I ravaged through my drawers looking for my best clothes. I found my favorite shirt, a blue-and-green plaid oxford I'd gotten from Gabriel Brothers a year ago for just a dollar because it was missing a button. My mom sewed one on. Good as new.

"Andy, can I borrow your hair gel?"

For five minutes, I played with my hair, hoping I had just the right amount. I slipped on my blue jeans and laced up my blue Puma sneakers.

"Am I wearing too much blue and green?" I asked.

"If you put on a yellow belt, you would look like the Brazilian flag."

That Wednesday evening, I took the long way, walking in front of the Cathedral of Learning and into South Oakland. Karen's brick apartment building was worn and drab—the opposite of how she looked that night, I would soon discover.

When Karen opened the door to her apartment, she dazzled me with her black dress and sandals. The dress hugged her body as if it had been made for her. Her bold eyebrows made her look like Audrey Hepburn in *Breakfast at Tiffany's*.

On the walk over, I asked Karen about what it was like in New York City. She seemed nervous. As we crossed the Cathedral lawn, I noticed the leaves were a mix of green, red, yellow, and orange. The fall air smelled like cinnamon and apples.

"Let's run across the lawn!" Karen exclaimed. Before I had a chance to answer, she grabbed my hand and we ran like kids through the grass and the crunchy leaves.

We made our way to Walnut Street, Shadyside's business district, a three-block stretch packed with coffee shops, restaurants, and boutiques. We walked up the steps to the second-floor entrance of Max & Erma's, where quirky artifacts like giant clown statues, oversized clocks, antique license plates, Indian carvings, and vintage Pittsburgh Pirates posters surrounded us. Romance City. We took a seat at the carved wooden bar and ordered up a round of Honey Brown Ales.

"Did things ever work out for you with football? Were you able to walk on?" she asked.

"Yes, I'm on the team," I said. "I'm the kicker."

She grabbed my arm. "You mean the starting kicker? Wow!"

I thought this was a good opportunity to try to impress her.

"You know, the kicker is the backbone of the team."

"The backbone?" She gave a throaty laugh and poked my thigh. "Come on, I grew up watching the Steelers every Sunday. Don't you think the quarterback is the backbone?"

I'd overreached. She was an Erie girl. Karen knew football. "Okay, I just meant that it's an important position."

We ordered up a second round of beers and continued to talk and laugh.

"What do you want to do now that you've graduated?" I asked.

"I just want to spin a globe with my eyes shut and stop it with my finger and go where that is. I want to travel and meet new people. I have a mantra: Life is about having as many new experiences and discovering as many new things as possible."

I scanned the bar and restaurant. We were the only ones left. It was 10:00 p.m. We had lost track of time. I asked her, "Do you want to head back and go to a Pitt bar? A lot of my friends are at Calico's tonight."

"I would love to."

Calico's was a dude ranch. The long bar was crawling with football players. In the large group, my friends were playing a game of darts. Lou and John were there.

"Kicker!" Lou shouted as we approached.

Also there was Mike, a defensive tackle. He engulfed me in a hug.

Mike Mohring, a jolly, giant teddy bear, tipped the scales at 6'5", 295 pounds. He went on to play five years in the NFL for the San Diego Chargers.

"Your friends make you look tiny," Karen said. It was true. At 6'1" and 190 pounds, I was dwarfed by many of my football buddies, who had blown out their pediatricians' height and weight charts.

My friends let Karen in on the dart melee. She showed no problem hanging with the guys.

About two hours later, I asked if she wanted to get out of there.

"Do you want to come back to my place?" Karen asked.

"Are you sure you don't want to drive two hours up to Erie for some fries and ranch dressing?" I teased.

She grabbed my hand, and we beelined it through the crowd for the front door, executing a successful "Irish goodbye." We walked the five blocks through South Oakland to her apartment, passing a couple of drunken kids and sidewalks littered with beer cans and empty pizza boxes.

Inside, the kitchen table, void of chairs, was graced with empty beer bottles and a half-eaten bowl of ramen. The light blue carpet was covered with cigarette burns and mystery stains. A hallway led to two bedrooms. The first belonged to her roomie, who was spending the night at her boyfriend's. Karen led me into the second.

Her tiny bedroom had a 12-inch, black-and-white TV with rabbit ears that sat on the faded green carpet next to a three-drawer black dresser. The walls were undecorated with the exception of a framed poster depicting a beautiful brunette painting her toenails while her shirtless ripped boyfriend sat in a chair watching her.

There was one place to sit: her twin bed that was pushed up against the wall. We sat side by side, and my heart quivered as we engaged in small talk about how she'd found the apartment, how cheap the rent was, and how nonexistent the landlord was.

"Let's put on some music," she said. "Do you like The Sundays?"

"I've never heard of them. But sure."

She slid a CD into the player, pressed play, and tuned the volume. When she returned to the bed, the space between our bodies had accidentally evaporated. Our hips and thighs seemed glued together. I felt a tingling jolt in my chest.

The first track started airy and light. Next, a clear and powerful female voice began to sing. The singer's voice was beautiful. In a sensual style, the singer delivered the lyrics: "Here's . . . where . . . the story ends." The phrase repeated again and again. *Ends?* I hope not.

Her boyfriend was gone, we'd been friends for over three years now, she seemed to trust me, *she'd* invited me back to her place and put on mood music. Maybe I should try to kiss her.

"What about you?" she was saying. "I've done most of the talking tonight. What do you want to do once you are done with school?"

We locked eyes. Why did she have to ask such a deep question right now?

"I want to play in the NFL." *And kiss you,* I thought.

And then Karen placed her hand on the side of my face and brushed her lips against mine. Karen pulled away and giggled. I caressed her hair as we kissed again. Our kiss lingered, and before we knew it The Sundays had stopped singing and 30 minutes had passed.

On my walk back up to my dorm, I imagined marrying her someday. Playing the loneliest position in sports didn't feel so lonely anymore.

• • •

We began talking and seeing each other almost every day. I started spending some of my nights at her place, and when I got back to my dorm one day after class, Andy had hung a "Missing Person" sign with a drawing of my face in the dorm lobby.

• • •

On Monday afternoon, as we began preparing for our sixth game of the season, against the Fighting Irish of Notre Dame, Coach Hackett gathered the team to vote for team captains. "I want you to think about the qualities of what it means to be a captain. Number one: leadership. Leading by example. Both on and off the field." He scanned the room, looking from player to player. "Number two: work ethic. A captain puts every ounce of effort into practice, weightlifting, and conditioning. Number three: mental toughness. He takes criticism from the coaches and implements it. He bounces back from his mistakes."

The assistant coaches handed out small pieces of paper and everyone wrote down their choices—one for offense, one for defense, and one for special teams. I was shocked when Coach Hackett announced the winners: "Gentlemen. I would like to announce your captains for the 1992 Pitt Panthers. Alex Van Pelt, Vernon Lewis, and Sean Conley."

After the meeting, Amos and I met to review game film and analyze my technique, but first he let me know what being a captain meant. "That was no fluke son, your teammates believe in you. They see how hard you work. They know you've made a believer out of Coach Hackett. I can't tell you how proud I am of you."

• • •

The next morning, I woke up in such excruciating pain that I couldn't get out of bed for classes. My back was spasming and locked up. *Shit*, I thought. Not this week, not right before Notre Dame.

I rolled off the side of the bed and crawled on my hands and knees, navigating through the minefield of Andy's boxers, moldy towels, *Rolling Stone* magazines, and video game controllers. I couldn't breathe. I felt pathetic.

There is, among young men in a locker room, a certain old-school denial about physical limitations. I didn't want to deal with an injury. I just assumed it would go away, but it didn't.

By that afternoon, I managed to get dressed and walk slowly over to the trainers' room. They gave me a script for 800 mg ibuprofen and Flexeril, a powerful muscle relaxant that made me sleepy.

I started doing an entire routine that included extra stretching with the help of the trainers, long soaks in the whirlpool, and regular applications of electrical stimulation and ice.

People don't expect kickers to be injured. The position is, however, highly susceptible to repetitive-use injury. You're overusing one side of your body in practice and in games. But you're not going to get a lot of pity from position players who risk brain and spinal injuries on any given play. That was fine because I had no plans to broadcast that I was injured, or how bad the pain was.

Division I football is a multi-billion-dollar business. Although the athletes don't get paid, there is a lot at stake. Most, like me, had hopes of going pro and scoring a bigger payday than any job we could get with a degree. But if you couldn't perform, you'd be buried on the bottom of the depth chart. Full-ride players who got injured sometimes never regained their starting positions. Walk-ons who showed up late for practice were often cut. In my case, if the coaches thought I was too injured to perform at my usual level, they'd bench me and I'd have nothing to show NFL scouts. So I did everything I could to keep my back problems on the down low.

That Thursday afternoon was our last practice of the week wearing pads. Near the end of practice, Coach Hackett announced that we were going to end with a field goal. Forty-five yards.

"Field goal team and field goal block team," Amos yelled.

As we jogged out onto the field, the stadium speakers started blaring the Notre Dame fight song. It was a tune I used to hum around my house as a kid. They'd been playing it all week during practice to piss us off. But now it was on full blast.

"It's the last play of the game and this is for the win. Make some noise!" Coach Hackett exclaimed.

My back pain was numbed from the pills. No problem. The ball sailed through the uprights. It was good.

Notre Dame would be a big test for both the team and me. They began the season ranked third in the country and had already demolished Michigan State and Purdue. That we were going to play them at home was little comfort. I was worried about how my back would hold up, and the rest of the team was just plain worried. If we were going to turn the season around, Notre Dame was the game to do it.

The night before the game, we followed our home game ritual, checking into the posh William Penn Hotel in downtown Pittsburgh. It was the team's way of avoiding any distractions. It was lights out promptly at 10:00 p.m.

As we drove into the parking lot the next day, I'd never seen so many tailgaters. The smell of burgers, sausages, and steaks grilling filled the bus as we made our way through a sea of royal blue and canary yellow. There was no small amount of Fighting Irish fans decked out in shamrock green scattered among the Pitt fans. The tailgaters paused to watch our bus drive by, led by cop cars with lights flashing.

We exited the bus, each of us dressed in our lucky suits or blazers. I wore my tartan wool red-and-black plaid sport coat that I'd scored from the Salvation Army. It clashed with my burnt-orange khaki pants and my one and only tie, a blue-and-green-striped silk tie that I'd gotten on sale from a J. Crew catalogue. My scratched, previously owned wingtips were one size too big.

My jersey with my last name sewn on the back was hanging inside my locker, looking freshly ironed. The equipment managers had laid out my pads and cleats, looking like they had never been used before.

A white short-sleeve shirt with "PITT" in blue script lay neatly folded on my chair, but today I needed something extra lucky. I pulled out of my backpack a raggy-looking T-shirt with a hole in one armpit and illegible blue-and-yellow letters on the front. I'd worn this shirt at practice when I first walked on to Pitt eight months ago.

"Put the music on!" a player shouted. The room was soon filled with the pulsing energy of Ice Cube and Dr. Dre. The music alternated between rap and rock. I never knew how or when it was decided who would be DJ, but there was never any arguing.

The music guy slipped in "Jump" by Kriss Kross and suddenly a climactic and infectious explosion of emotions kicked in. Guys started jumping and hollering. A player tossed a thigh pad and hit a linebacker right in the face. The most storied college football program in history was down the hall in the visitors' locker room, the only team in college football with their own TV network deal. Yet in that moment, the tension dissipated, replaced with exhilaration. For a fleeting moment, we were no longer thinking of what lay ahead of us. We were just enjoying the ride.

I unzipped a side pocket in my backpack and grabbed an orange-tinted bottle of prescription pills: Cyclobenzaprine, a muscle relaxant. I broke one tiny pill in half, placed it in my mouth, and swallowed. I thought, *Please work. No muscle spasms tonight.* Then I headed down the hall to the trainers' room.

Sitting in front of my locker, I thought of the dozens of NFL scouts that would be in the stands tonight. Relax. It's just another game. Another kick. I've done this before.

More than the scouts, I wanted to impress Karen, who was stuck watching on TV while she waitressed in the bar.

• • •

The team fed off the energy of our home crowd. On our first offensive possession, we drove deep into Irish territory. However, we couldn't punch it into the end zone. I kicked a 20-yard field goal to give Pitt a 3–0 lead. Just a minute later, Jerome Bettis rolled into the end zone from eight yards out. 7–3 Notre Dame.

Late in the first quarter, it was fourth down on the Notre Dame 31 yard line. Forty-eight-yard field goal attempt. I told myself to do exactly the same thing I'd been doing. Three steps back, step and a half over. I'd visualized this moment before.

I trusted Lou to snap the ball lightning quick. I trusted J. R. to catch the ball and place it down swiftly and spin the laces to face the goalposts. I trusted the offensive lineman to give me just over one second to get the kick off my foot. We needed another score to keep our confidence that we could hang with the star-studded Irish.

I nodded to J. R. that I was ready. I hit the ball. Before I looked up, I knew it was going to be good.

It cleared the crossbar with ease. The Pitt student section exploded with dancing pompoms, and the Pitt band started jamming the school's fight song. It would have been good from over 60 yards. J. R. hugged me, and there were high fives all around. The five-second celebration was over. As I jogged over to the sideline, a wave of emotions filled me. Everything happened so fast.

For the first time, I felt like I was really on the team. Something bigger than myself.

Once at the sideline, Amos acted like it was just another day in the park.

"Good kick, son."

And, before I knew it, it was time for the next kick.

As I headed out for the kickoff, I felt a sense of ease. I could do this. I'm in a flow now. Ease. It was fun. Gone was the fear of "the next one." I couldn't wait for "the next one."

We kept it close into the third quarter, but then Jerome Bettis ran 50 yards for a touchdown, taking the wind out of our sails. We lost 52–21.

Back in the locker room, everyone was subdued, thinking of what could have been. If that play or that one drive had succeeded, maybe the game would have gone the other way. Inside my head, other thoughts were rattling around. Given the high profile of the game, I couldn't help but wonder if any NFL scouts had seen me kick. I hoped Karen had seen it.

CHAPTER 9
TWO MINUTE WARNING

"We can't let the Missile touch the ball," Amos said at the special teams meeting at the hotel the night before the game against Syracuse. I repeated that phrase in my head when I went to bed and woke up with it. *Don't let the Missile touch the ball. Don't let the Missile touch the ball. Don't let the Missile touch the ball.*

The Missile's real name was Qadry Ismail. He was named First Team All-America kick returner in 1991 and had already amassed over 2,000 career yards in kick returns. Teams did everything they could to prevent him from touching the ball on kickoffs and punts, including kicking the ball out of bounds, sky kicks, which forced an opponent to call a fair catch, and squib kicks, which bounced haphazardly down the field, throwing off the return team.

Amos's strategy was simple. "Kick it over the Missile's head, son." He trusted that I would be able to.

The strategy had a safety measure installed. When I lined up to kick off, I would spot the location of the Missile. Whether he was on the right or left side of the goal line, I would kick it to the opposite side. I would show my teammates where I was kicking it by rubbing one side of my helmet. Tricky.

We were in Syracuse, New York, in the Carrier Dome on Halloween. The stadium was packed, as Syracuse was the 12th-ranked team in the country.

I connected on a 46-yard field goal to get us started, and then got ready to place the ball as far from the Missile as humanly possible.

I lined up eight yards from the tee and looked down the field. The Missile was on the left, bouncing on his feet like Muhammad Ali getting ready for a heavyweight title fight. I tapped the right side of my helmet. I looked at the right-hand corner of the end zone. That was my target. I was going to kick it deep and *right*.

As I kicked the ball, something didn't feel right. I'd closed my hips too much. I watched the ball go high and deep, but straight down the middle. The Missile shuffled a step or two to his left and caught the ball on the goal line. "Damn," I thought, "He was right under it."

Unfortunately, my teammates were racing toward the right side of the end zone, where they were forced into a cluster by Syracuse's blockers. The Missile saw an open lane and dashed upfield slanting to his right, like he'd just been fired out of a cannon. There was mostly open green in front of him. I stood at midfield, the lone safety valve in our Missile defense system.

He ran straight at me, fearless. Kickers are not respected as tacklers, and he was playing chicken with me. My mind raced, searching for any memory of a tackling drill. The only thought I could come up with was "Stay light on your feet," but my mismatched cleats felt like they were stuck in wet cement. At the last second, he deked me. Right before colliding head on, he juked to my left and was by me before I could lunge to grab an armful of air. I tumbled gracelessly to the turf, watching helplessly as our own super speedster Jay Jones ran down the Missile three yards shy of the Pitt end zone.

The 41–10 loss would include Alex Van Pelt literally being knocked out on a sack play, and out for the rest of the game.

I had a bad habit of making tough situations worse. Just off the bus from Syracuse, I was in no mood to be good company. Karen and I had made plans to meet up at a bar named Zelda's that had a cheap drink special in honor of Halloween. Mad at the world, I left the bar before she got there. But everywhere I went, the TVs were tuned to ESPN's game of the week, and during breaks in the broadcast, they kept showing the clip of the Missile's kick return and my clumsy attempt to tackle him. My mood grew darker. At the third bar of the night, around 1:00 a.m., I ran into Karen's roommate, Dina.

"Karen is pissed. She dressed up as Catwoman."

"Catwoman?" The image of what she would look like in a tight leather outfit popped into my head. Followed quickly by profound regret.

"Yep. You blew it."

Andy stood next to me, shaking his head. "You're a fucking idiot."

Back in my dorm room, I found a message on my answering machine. "Hi Sean, it's Karen. I went to meet you at Zelda's tonight and . . . you blew me off. Umm, okay. Call me."

That, in a nutshell, is how it feels to be two feet tall.

When I called her the next day, she started with, "Oh, the games we play." For years afterwards, "Oh, the games we play," would be code, another way of saying, "Sean's an idiot."

• • •

Our last home game of the season was against Louisville on November 14. It was Senior Day, my last college home game ever.

Coach Hackett seemed tired during his pregame speech. We'd heard rumors that the administration was considering firing him. Local sportswriters were bashing him. Expectations at Pitt were high. The team was expected to go to a bowl game every year. The last one Pitt had made it to, the Sun Bowl in El Paso, Texas, had been in 1989. We had enough talent, but there were a lot of injuries and something just wasn't clicking. Any hope of a bowl game was long since dead.

The day was cold, windy, and dreary. Many fans had lost their patience. Some had brought signs that said, "I can't HACK-IT." The boo-birds were out in full force, and it made us feel bitter and confused. The announcer said over the PA that there were 14,065 people in the seats of the stadium that could hold almost 56,000 fans. It was a stark difference from the Notre Dame game a few weeks before.

My parents were in their usual spot in the parents sections. Karen sat in the top row at the 40 yard line with Andy. A freezing rain drizzled throughout the game. I made another field goal but we went out with a whimper, losing 31–16.

Our second-to-last game was at Penn State in a steady downpour. The field resembled a mushy cow pasture; players slipped and fell and our white road jerseys were covered in mud by the second quarter. My kickoffs, which typically found the end zone, were landing at the five. I thought it might just be the condition of the field, but as the game went on, each time I kicked the ball I felt lightning bolts of pain run up the front of my leg. My mystery injury was affecting my strength, and no painkillers could help that.

I did my best to hide the extent of my suffering. It was my last chance to get the NFL scouts to notice me. I was afraid to ask for time off during the week to rest my leg, too, because I didn't want Amos to think I was "soft."

I wasn't alone in this playing-through-pain thing. The practice was implicitly condoned and even encouraged. In the early 90s, even when you took a blow to your head, like Alex Van Pelt did against Syracuse—known as "getting your bell rung"—they'd just give you some smelling salts and toss you back in the game if you *seemed* okay, disregarding the risk of concussion. Today, after years of ignoring and denying concussion evidence, the NFL has recently begun introducing measures aimed at reducing brain injuries.

Amos found me again in the training room as I was lying on my belly getting heat on my low back.

"Hey son, back spasms again?"

"It's fine."

"Don't piss on my leg and tell me it's raining."

After a moment of figuring out what that meant, and trying to keep a straight face, I responded, "Okay, it hurts like hell at times. And I could probably use some rest."

"Why didn't you tell me this earlier?"

"I was worried you would bench me," I admitted.

"Bench you? You're one of the best damn kickers in the country. I don't want to see you kick another ball until you feel it's time."

Fortunately, Karen was more forgiving than most people would have been and our relationship continued past the Halloween stumble. That meant I had someone to lean on as our season crashed and burned.

Coach Hackett was fired right before we played our last game, at Hawaii. That meant the whole coaching staff was likely on the chopping block. Not great for morale. The standard operating procedure when a D-I coach gets fired is to clean house and get rid of all the other coaches as well, because any new head coach coming in will want to assemble his own staff that operates according to his particular philosophy and strategies.

On the flight out to Hawaii, I sat in front of Amos and his wife. I had taken two Flexerils and was slowly fading. But before I went under, I was treated to a dose of what being an adult in the world of high-stakes football could be like: the unknowns, uncertainty, stress, and fleeting nature of the business. Amos's wife, Stacy, tried to whisper, but I could still hear her. Amos and Stacy had been in Pittsburgh for only one year. Before that, they'd been in Alabama—and before that, Philadelphia.

"What are we going to do if they fire you? Are we going to have to move again?" They had a two-year-old daughter.

Amos sighed heavily. "Unless they hire Sal after this game. Yeah, they'll let all of us go." The linebackers' coach, Sal Sunseri, had been made the interim coach in place of Hackett.

"I don't want to move again. I don't want to go through this again."

"It'll be okay, I promise. We'll land on our feet. I'll find something."

My parents, who came to every game including those on the road, couldn't afford the trip, and because the game wasn't broadcast in Erie, they decided to drive to Pittsburgh to watch from a Holiday Inn.

Five minutes after taking the Flexeril, I was out cold. When I woke up, 10 hours had passed and a woman wearing a Hawaiian dress was placing a lei around my head while men played the ukulele.

Sal Sunseri had been a walk-on at Pitt himself in 1978 and became a First Team All-America linebacker. The Pittsburgh Steelers had drafted him, but a knee injury during training camp ended his career.

Coach Sal had always wanted the Pitt head coach job, and finally his moment had arrived. The pregame speech was like something out of the movies. He jumped around like John Belushi, shouting things like, "You have to play today like someone just hit your mom with a baseball bat!" Then he tossed the chalkboard across the room. We tore out of the locker room like banshees.

Inspired by Coach Sal, the team played with the most energy we'd had all season, but after three quarters, we ran out of gas.

Late in the game, a Hawaii player right in front of me on the sideline hit one of our players. A year full of frustration was unleashed. We had a bench-clearing brawl. Punching guys wearing pads, I discovered, was highly ineffective. The melee lasted for about a minute, and then order was restored.

Despite this chaos, my kickoffs flew into the back of the end zone; one nearly went through the goalposts. And I made another field goal, my 16th of the season.

I flew back to Pittsburgh with a wooden Hawaiian Tiki God of Happiness in my bag for my grandma.

I finished my season having made 16 out of 19 field goal attempts. I was named First Team Associated Press All-East Team, and First Team All–Academic Big East, and I received an Athlete Scholar Award from Pitt. I was nominated for the Lou Groza, the award given to the nation's top kicker. Pretty good for my first year as a Division I athlete.

But the individual awards and success had an empty feeling since the team finished with just three wins.

A few days later, Amos called me into his office. I walked as slowly as I could down to the stadium. I wanted to delay the inevitable.

When I walked in, half of his office was already packed. He had his family photos in a box. My heart sank and I felt my body tense up. He told me that he, along with a number of the other coaches, had already been fired.

"Someday we'll have a beer and laugh about all this," he said. Standing there, at 22, it didn't seem likely to me. I asked about his job prospects and he told me he felt confident that he would pick up something. He seemed calm, or at least resolved. I hugged him and thanked him for all that he had done for me. Amos had been my father away from home. It's rare to find a mentor who gives you unconditional support, someone who believes in you even when you doubt yourself. I knew I'd see Amos again, but it wouldn't be like having him there on the field with me. I was going to be alone again, and I could only hope that Amos would find a job that made sense for him and his family.

As I told him how much of a difference he'd made for me, his eyes began to well up. I felt a lump in my throat.

"Coaching you, son, made it all worth it for me," he said.

Many years after that final meeting, I was listening to the local sports radio station in my car when the announcer said: "And the Steelers have a new special teams coach, Amos Jones." Since we'd parted ways in 1992, his coaching adventures had taken him to Eau Gallie High School in Florida, Tulane University, the British Columbia Lions of the Canadian Football League, East St. John's High School in Louisiana, University of Cincinnati, James Madison University, Mississippi State, and then back to Pittsburgh, with the Steelers.

We had that big reunion he'd predicted at the Steelers' training facility. He took me around introducing me to the other coaches, including Head Coach Mike Tomlin, and to the players who walked by. Later that evening, our families had dinner together and we had that beer.

• • •

I decided to look for an agent. An NFL agent is someone who helps market your name to NFL teams and then, if you're lucky enough to be drafted, helps negotiate your contract. The agent typically receives 3 percent of your salary once the regular season begins. Scouts and agents cannot communicate with players until they have completed their final collegiate season.

Unfortunately, the firings hadn't been bad news just for the coaches; they meant that the seniors on the team were left adrift. Normally, a Division I coaching staff provides advice, counsel, and direction to seniors looking to go pro, as well as serving as go-betweens with pro scouts and NFL teams. The coaching staff can, in their way, work as hard to set up graduating players with exposure to pro teams as they do recruiting high school players. After all, the more players that go pro out of a program, the more prestige shines back on the college team. But with no coaching staff in place, any Pitt prospect had to fend for himself.

Getting representation is, even under the best circumstances, an uphill battle. A small number of elite pro prospects—like my Pitt teammate Curtis Martin (who went on to become the fourth all-time NFL rusher and inducted into the Hall of Fame)—will be blasted by multiple high-profile agents looking to represent them. But the vast majority of players like me struggle to sign with an agent. Players looking at league minimum if anything are just not worth most agents' time because the commission will be so small. I called every agent I could. I'd tell them I was a kicker, what my stats were, and not much else. They'd hang up without so much as a kind word. Often, I didn't make it past the word *kicker* as they were among the lowest-paid positions with the least number of jobs.

Every Division I program has a "Pro Day" to show off graduating talent. It gives NFL scouts a chance to see all the school's prospects at one time. The Pitt Pro Day was a poor showing.

On a cold day in late March, the seniors dreaming of the NFL, about 15 of us, warmed up in our Pitt practice gear. As we jogged on the green turf, played catch, and stretched, we kept our eye on the growing number of visitors walking into the Cost Center. Scouts in their NFL team jackets began to gather around the field with their stopwatches, clipboards, pens, and nametags looking for potential investments.

But, with no coaching staff, we were leaderless, we had no voice to promote us, and it looked as if just 16 or 17 NFL scouts were there. Which meant about 10 teams hadn't shown up.

The scouts began to work out the seniors from their list of potential draft picks, using stopwatches to time their 40-yard dash speeds and watching them do agility drills. During the short breaks in action, I introduced myself to some of the scouts and asked them if they'd be interested in watching me kick for a few minutes before they left. A few responded, "If I have time."

Time came and went, and they all left—and I stood there holding my ball bag over my shoulder like a kid ditched at the playground.

Before I took off, I decided that if I wasn't getting a look from the NFL today, maybe I could at least get an agent. I saw a man in a shiny pink tracksuit talking to one of my teammates; he looked like he *had* to be an agent.

I approached him and said, "Excuse me, are you an agent?"

In a heavy Brooklyn accent, he said, "No, I'm just a friend of Jeff's." Jeff was a senior for Pitt working out at Pro Day. "I'm helping him contact NFL teams. My name is Jimmy Lozano."

There was no getting around the fact that he seemed shady, like a local wiseguy who had found work as an extra on *The Sopranos*. Desperation forgives many flaws.

"So you *are* an agent?" I asked.

"Well, I guess I am now. Jeff's my first client."

"Would you be interested in a second?"

"I'll give you my number. Call me tomorrow and we can talk."

I called the next day, shared my resume with him, and we signed a contract. But I got the sense that I was still on my own, because Jimmy had never been an agent before, so I decided to market myself as well.

I went to the Pitt football offices in search of Les Banos, the team photographer and video man. His office was filled with an endless array of cameras, tapes, and tripods. I explained my situation and the urgency.

"Sean, of course I can help. Anything is possible."

Helping and believing were what Les did and lived. A spry man in his late 50s who spoke with a Hungarian accent, he had a gentle soul and was revered by everyone who knew him. Les stood as high as my shoulders, but his courage and heart always made him seem huge to me. During World War II, while the Germans occupied his homeland, he was a spy for the OSS (a predecessor of the Central Intelligence Agency). He operated undercover in the Hungarian division of the SS, interacting with high-ranking German officers including Adolf Eichmann. He successfully hid Jews in, among other places, a factory's sewer system, saving many of them from the concentration camps.

Thanks to Les and his assistant, I ended up with 28 copies of a highlight reel of me on VHS—one for every NFL team.

Next, I met John at the library. After combing through the reference section, we found a book that listed the phone numbers and addresses of each NFL team. I sent a tape to each team along with a one-page letter including my statistics and awards.

I waited a few days, and then followed up with each and every special teams coach in the NFL. I tried to sell them on my skills, and expressed my desire to have the opportunity to play for them. Between classes, I went down the list and made long-distance phone calls. *My mom is going to kill me*, I thought.

One afternoon, just as I hung up with the Dallas Cowboys after they told me they already had another kicker in mind, Andy walked in with a small bag of groceries from the 7-Eleven and a Slim Jim in his mouth. The phone rang and he reached over and grabbed the receiver before I had a chance.

"Hello?" Andy said with the Slim Jim still dangling in his mouth. "Sure, just a second." He lowered the receiver. "It's some director of something guy named Rooney with the New York Giants."

"Don't mess with me, asshole."

"I'm not shitting you."

It was probably Karen or my dad.

"Hello?" I stared at Andy to see his expression.

"Sean. This is Tim Rooney, I'm the director of pro personnel with the New York Giants."

I stopped breathing for a moment and put my right hand on my head. I silently mouthed to Andy, "It's the New York Giants."

He mouthed back, "No shit, Sherlock." Then he walked over and put his arm around me and his ear next to the receiver to try to listen in.

"I'm looking right now at the tape you sent us. I'm really impressed. I'd like to come and visit you at Pitt next week and work you out privately."

I had three days to get ready. My leg and back craved rest, but I was sure I couldn't take even a moment's pause. Instead, I trained hard each day leading up to the workout. My kicks were up and down like the Dow Jones. Some kickoffs would fly into the end zone, and some came up short, landing on the 10 yard line.

The night before my workout, I went to bed early to rest up. I prayed that my leg would somehow be strong and full of stamina when the Giants arrived. But on the morning of the workout, my lower back felt locked up. I loaded up on ibuprofen and muscle relaxants. I needed a big day. I had only moments to impress with little room for error.

When I walked into the football offices at 10:00 a.m., it was eerily quiet. All the coaches were now out looking for new jobs. Debbie, the administrative assistant, told me Mr. Rooney was in Amos's old office watching video.

All that remained in there was a desk, a couple of chairs, a TV, and a remote. Gone were Amos's pictures of his family. Rooney was sitting in Amos's chair, which gave me a heavy feeling in my stomach. A pile of VCR tapes was on the desk. He had a notebook in hand, its pages covered with scribble that I could not decipher.

"I've been here since about 8:00 a.m. I've seen every kick of yours from this season," he said. "You had a great year. Are you ready?"

As we made our way to the field, he peppered me with questions about my season, how I handled pressure, and how my grades were.

His son, whom he brought along to be the ball boy, opened up a royal blue New York Giants ball bag and poured four balls stamped with the NFL logo onto the green turf. John had volunteered to hold and Lou handled the snaps. He met us at the field and the workout was underway.

I kicked five field goals from 25 yards and then worked back to 55. My accuracy was dead on and I made almost all of them.

Kickoffs were next.

"Let's do 10," he said.

I began pleading for my leg to hang in there. Ten more. That's it.

The first six or seven kicks found the end zone. But my leg strength went on a surprise vacation, and the last few landed around the five.

The final three kicks were not quite NFL Draft material, and I knew it.

"Okay, I think we're good," he said.

His son helped me pick up my balls and we walked out of the empty stadium together.

"I'm going to be honest with you."

I prepared myself for the worst.

"We're not going to draft you, but I've looked at over 30 kickers who are eligible for the draft. Right now, I would put you the third best. So someone else might take you in the late rounds or sign you as a free agent."

I had wanted so badly for him to say that the Giants might draft me. I was upset that my leg strength wasn't there today. But third best out of 30. I would take that.

Suddenly, I couldn't wait for the draft.

"Keep these balls to train with."

He shook my hand and left.

The chances of successfully making the jump from college to the NFL as a kicker are slim. In 1993, the NFL had 28 teams. Each team carried just one kicker. There is no "backup kicker": 28 teams, 28 jobs for kickers. That's just 28 positions in the entire world for what I do. To compound the difficulty, in a given year, just two to three teams are looking to replace their kickers. Two to three open jobs. And each year about 20 lucky college kickers sign contracts with NFL teams to come into training camp and compete for these precious rare spots. But I knew I belonged in one of those positions.

A couple of weeks later, on draft day, April 25, Jimmy called me from his house in Sunrise, Florida.

"I just talked to the New England Patriots," he said. "They told me, if you're available in later rounds, they'd probably draft you. I spoke with other teams who needed kickers too, including Tampa Bay and Cincinnati, and they all told me that they have you in the top three on their board. So the odds are looking good!"

Teams create draft boards, in which they rank players by position. According to Jimmy, most teams had me in the top three on most draft boards, just like what Rooney from the Giants said. It was happening. A momentary sense of calm filled my head. The video I'd sent out to each team must have worked.

The first day of the draft was uneventful for me; they just completed round one. Rick Mirer, the captain of Notre Dame, was picked number two by the Seattle Seahawks. Jerome Bettis, the running back with thighs the size of tree trunks, was picked number 10 by the Los Angeles Rams. He would later be inducted into the Hall of Fame in 2015. Day two, which would include rounds two through eight, would be the pivotal day for me, as most kickers didn't get drafted until the late rounds.

I skipped classes for the second day of the draft and parked myself next to the phone in my dorm room and turned on ESPN. I just wanted to be alone in case it didn't go my way. A familiar name was called. The NFL commissioner said from the podium, "With the 52nd pick of the 1993 NFL Draft, the Minnesota Vikings select Qadry Ismail." The Missile. I had a fleeting moment of satisfaction that people I had played against were going to play in the NFL. But I wanted in the club as well.

I didn't care which team drafted me. I was no longer a fan rooting for a specific team and jersey colors, I just wanted to be on a team.

Every time the phone rang, I didn't know if it was a team or Jimmy, my dad, Karen, or my friends checking in.

When the fifth round began, I stared hard at the phone. From the fifth through the eighth was my chance. Five picks into the fifth round, it rang.

It was Jimmy.

"I just talked with New England," he said. "They said they will probably take you with their next pick. Get ready."

When the time came for New England's pick, the ESPN announcer said, "The New England Patriots select kicker Scott Sisson from Georgia Tech."

Ouch. But there were still plenty of picks left. And if the Patriots had come close to drafting me, someone else might. I had to be next.

Sixth round. No call.

Picks kept coming and going. And as the draft wore down, so did my hopes.

Seventh round. No call.

The eighth and final round began. It was evening now; the draft day was about eight hours old.

The phone rang.

"I just talked with the Cincinnati Bengals and Tampa Bay," Jimmy said. "They've both said they will take you with their picks. Hang in there."

The scroll moved across the bottom of the screen on ESPN. It read, "The Bengals, with the 202nd pick of the NFL Draft, select kicker Doug Pelfrey from Kentucky."

Who's that? I thought.

Every time I heard another kicker's name, I felt envy, jealousy, and anger wash over me.

There was a pit in my stomach. I felt like an idiot and was glad I had chosen to watch this alone.

Only one pick remained. Pick number 224. Tampa Bay.

It was time. The final pick, known as Mr. Irrelevant. The announcer spoke.

"Tampa Bay selects kicker . . . Daron Alcorn from Akron."

Another name I didn't recognize. I was overcome with white-hot anger. Then agony. How could this have happened? I thought back to the thousands of hours kicking, the weights, the pain. All for nothing.

The draft was over. And my career seemed over, too. I sat at my desk hunched over, frozen, numb, staring at the phone in disbelief.

I buried my face in my hands. I expected that it was a mistake, and any minute, a team would be calling to say I was their pick. Then the phone rang.

It was Jimmy. "I'm really sorry, Sean. I don't know what happened. Everyone I spoke with had you really high. It's a numbers game."

Before we hung up, he reminded me it wasn't over yet. A team could still call and sign me as an undrafted free agent. After the draft, depending on roster size, each team signs about 12 rookies who weren't drafted.

While I sat by the phone and waited, I started cursing myself for waiting so long to go to Pitt. If only I had transferred earlier, the NFL would have seen me play more. It was so easy to second-guess every college career choice I had ever made, to dwell on how things might have been. I knew I was better than some of the kickers picked ahead of me. Why hadn't I trained harder? What would Karen think of me? I could have made my parents proud, but instead I'd failed.

The undrafted free agency was a fast process. By the end of the night, teams would have filled most of those spots. I decided I would sit by the phone for another 30 minutes. After that, I had to let it go.

The phone rang again.

"Hi Sean." It was my dad. He had been watching the draft on ESPN at home. He called to let me know that he and my mom knew I hadn't been drafted, and they were still proud of me.

"Thanks, Dad," I said. "I gotta go, just in case someone calls me to be a free agent."

The phone rang again.

"Hey dude, did you get drafted?" Andy said from a campus phone.

"No," I said.

"Fuck it. The NFL is dumb anyways. Why don't you come down to C. J.'s and get wasted?"

I told him I'd think about it.

Seven o'clock came and darkness set in. It wasn't supposed to end like this. *There must be a way that I still have a chance. This isn't over. It can't be.*

I grabbed my jacket and some $1 bills and loose change. The phone rang. I figured it had to be Jimmy again.

"Hi Sean, this is Kevin Colbert from the Detroit Lions," he said in a raspy voice.

I pumped my fist to my empty room as I gripped the phone tighter.

"Hello, Mr. Colbert," I said as calmly as I could, then bit my lip as I listened.

"I'm glad I got you. We'd like to bring you in as a free agent."

So this was ecstasy. I went from wanting to throw my textbooks at the wall to tears of joy rolling down my face. All of the hard work, pain, and ups and downs that I had gone through had finally brought me to the moment I had always dreamed of.

I was going to play in the NFL.

"I was at Pitt Stadium when you played Notre Dame. I was impressed with your ability, especially the long field goal you made and your kickoff strength," he continued.

I looked out the window at the stadium where it all happened.

He assured me that I would get into at least one preseason game so that I could have some film to show other teams if I got cut by the Lions. Before he hung up, he said I would be getting more calls from some teams.

"Take a few days to see what's out there for you, and then get back to us. We will wait."

I hung up the phone and yelled to an empty room, "I'm a Detroit Lion!"

I fell to my knees. *Okay,* I thought. *Calm down.*

What did he mean by "probably get a few more calls?" My thoughts became jumbled. I could be a Detroit Lion right now but he was saying I could wait and see if I could find a better fit. I was too excited to think straight. I was dying to tell someone—my parents, Andy, Karen at C. J.'s.—but I couldn't tie up the line. I had to just stay by myself next to the phone.

I decided to wait about an hour before meeting Andy and Karen to see if Kevin Colbert could see into the future like Nostradamus. It turned out he could. The phone rang again.

"Hi Sean, this is Pete Rodriguez. I'm the special teams coach with the Phoenix Cardinals. We'd like to fly you in next week for a kicking competition with another college kicker. Whoever does the best will be offered a free agent contract."

I told Coach Rodriguez I had an offer from Detroit already, but that I'd get back to him really soon. Two minutes later, the phone rang again.

"Hi Sean, this is Charles Bailey from the Pittsburgh Steelers."

I danced in place. *The Steelers.*

"We'd like you to come down to Three Rivers Stadium tomorrow to see you kick in person."

My entire body quivered. I was speechless.

"Thank you. I will be there."

I called my parents and told them the news in a one-minute speed call. My mom cried. My dad didn't know what to say. I called Jimmy and he sounded like he was going to cry too.

After hanging up with Jimmy, I thought, I have three offers, I don't need any more. If someone calls, it will only make it more confusing. I closed the door and heard a ring from inside my room. I cracked open the door and watched the phone vibrate as it rang, then decided, *It's time to party.*

I floated down the hill to see Karen and Andy at the bar. When I walked in, Karen approached me and gave me a hug that lasted longer than normal. She looked up at me and her brown eyes looked heavy. "I'm so sorry you didn't get drafted." And she hugged me even tighter.

"I just got an offer from the Lions. The Cardinals and the Steelers called too!"

"What?"

She jumped up into my arms, wrapping her legs around my waist. She kissed me hard, like she was the one who had just gotten signed to the NFL. I set her down, and as we locked eyes, I realized this woman was as invested in me as I was in her. She cared. My dream of a pro career wasn't unrealistic to her. It wasn't pie in the sky. It was something I believed in, so she believed in it too because she saw us as "we." As someone who had spent a lot of lonely hours staring at goalposts, it was amazing to think that someone so incredible had my back. I really wasn't in it alone. Before either of us could say anything else, the owner of the bar, C. J., rolled up on us. "Karen, what's going on here?"

"He's going to the NFL!"

"Congratulations. Give him a free beer and get back to work."

• • •

I didn't get much sleep that night. I spent most of the evening thinking of the possibilities. I had three chances to sign a free agent contract. The NFL was about to happen, and I just wanted to sign and make it official. They didn't have to pay me a dime.

In the morning, John picked me up and drove me to Three Rivers Stadium on Pittsburgh's North Side. We parked in the oversized lot next to the Allegheny River, then got out of the car and just stared at the imposing stadium for a moment. My hands were sweaty and I had a fluttery feeling in my stomach.

"This is crazy," John said. He didn't move. "The Pittsburgh friggin' Steelers. Three Rivers Stadium."

"Hey man, let's go," I said.

John told me it's destiny. "You walk on to Pitt. No one gives you a chance. A year later, you're a Pittsburgh Steeler."

I smiled.

Inside, we looked in awe at the display cases of Super Bowl trophies and the framed pictures of former and current Steeler greats. As a kid, I'd been a Cleveland Browns fan, rooting *against* the Steelers. And now, I wanted to play for them. I didn't feel like a football fan anymore. I wanted in the big show.

In the locker room, I geared up and got ready for the workout.

Walking out onto the stadium turf was surreal. I was walking on the same field as NFL greats like Terry Bradshaw and Lynn Swann. It was the same field where the Pirates' Roberto Clemente had circled the bases to capacity crowds. Today, the stadium seats were empty. A handful of coaches watched me compete against a kicker from North Carolina.

The coaches kept track of our made and missed kicks while Bill Cowher, the head coach, nicknamed "The Chin" and known for his spit-spewing tirades, receding hairline, tight mustache, and imposing jaw, looked on in silence from a short distance away.

I was in the zone. I made almost all of my kicks, and my kickoffs all found the end zone.

At the end of the workout, one of the coaches approached me and said, "Coach Cowher wants to see you in his office."

Holy shit. This sounded much better than grade school, when *the principal* wanted to see me in the office.

He walked me there and closed the door behind me, leaving me alone with Coach Cowher. At 35, he was the youngest coach in the NFL. His office was filled with books, plaques, and proudly displayed pictures of his wife and daughters. He stood up and gave me a firm handshake.

"Thanks for coming down today," he said in a boisterous voice.

All I could think as I sat across from him at his sprawling desk, looking at him in disbelief, was, *That's Bill Cowher.*

He asked questions in rapid fire—at first, none of them about football. "Where are you from? What are you studying at Pitt?"

I told him I remembered him from when I was a little kid, watching him play for my favorite team at the time, the Cleveland Browns. His entire body moved when he talked. He spoke almost as if he were my friend, more than a coach.

After about five or 10 minutes, he shifted gears.

"Hey, I liked what I saw out there. You have an NFL leg and you seem levelheaded and poised." He paused. "With our current roster numbers, I won't know until June if we'll have space for you in camp."

June. My mind raced. *I can't wait till June.*

"Tell me what other free agent options you have," he said.

"Detroit already offered me a contract; they also promised me playing time during the preseason, and Phoenix asked me to come out for a kicking competition before they'll consider signing me."

"Detroit offered you a contract and playing time?"

"Yes, Kevin Colbert did."

"Go to Detroit," he advised. "You can't pass up an opportunity to get playing time and game film. That's the most important thing for a rookie."

I was sad for a hot second—I would not be a Pittsburgh Steeler—but at the same time, I was excited because by the end of the day, I was going to be a Detroit Lion.

Waiting in the lobby, looking at the case holding the shining Super Bowl trophies was John, looking happier than a kid on Christmas morning.

"You're smiling; are you a fucking Steeler? What did Coach Cowher say?"

"Nope, I'm going to sign with Detroit right now."

I couldn't get to my phone fast enough. I called Phoenix and thanked them for the offer but said I had to pass. Then I punched in the numbers for Detroit. When the secretary answered, I asked for Kevin Colbert.

"Hi, Mr. Colbert. This is Sean Conley. I would be honored to sign with the Detroit Lions."

• • •

There was no time to enjoy the moment. It was May, and I had three months to prepare for training camp. I went into overdrive. Karen, busting my balls, asked me each morning of that summer what I had to do that day, knowing my answer would always be the same.

"Kick and lift." No days off.

I moved into an apartment with three other Pitt football players. I only ever saw it by daylight, because I spent almost every night at Karen's apartment, which was the Ritz compared to the dump I had.

Karen busted her ass that summer waitressing at C. J.'s. I was 12 credits shy of graduating, so I took two classes and made special arrangements with the professors to make up for my missing attendance when I would be leaving for Detroit in July.

One afternoon, Karen walked into my apartment and told me that the wife of the Steelers' kicker Gary Anderson had been in her kickboxing class that day. "And I got his phone number for you," she added.

With Amos now coaching at a high school in Florida, I was coachless and in need of some guidance. I decided to reach out to Gary Anderson.

He was originally from South Africa and, like me, was a former soccer player. I called him up to introduce myself, and after some friendly conversation and some kicker talk, I asked if he'd like to kick together for a day or two.

"Sean," Gary replied in his smooth South African accent, "I'm sorry, but during the summer, I *rest* my body and save myself for the season."

What did he just say? He took time off to *rest*? Not just a weekend, but a whole summer? *What a lazy dude*, I thought. I wished him luck with the upcoming season, and that was that.

Gary Anderson was, at that time, already a 10-year veteran and an accomplished player. Despite my initial judgment, as I sat on Karen's couch mulling it over, I figured he must know something I didn't know. No successful NFL player was simply lazy. *Rest*. It was an interesting concept. Maybe I should consider this foreign idea of "rest" as well?

After that talk with Gary, I thought about my mystery ailment and decided to scale down my kicking to every other day and no more than 30 to 40 kicks per day. Compared to the way Gary, an experienced professional, trained, however, I was still doing far too much.

CHAPTER 10
TRAINING CAMP

"Welcome to Detroit, men," Wayne Fontes said.

The Detroit Lions' head coach stood at the front of a large room in the Pontiac Silverdome, the home of the Lions, speaking of the training camp about to begin. His voice was smooth with a slight accent passed down from his Portuguese father; it went well with his tanned leathery skin and a furrowed brow.

I was an NFL player. It sounded right. That's who I was now. I'd been telling myself it would happen for 15 years. Part of me believed it. Part of me thought I was in a dream.

The auditorium-style classroom was filled with over 100 players, coaches, and staff members. The veterans who sat in the front appeared relaxed and laughed at his quips. I sat up at attention in the back with the other rookies. I spotted living legend running back Barry Sanders. In just four seasons in the NFL, Sanders had already amassed almost 6,000 yards running the football, and he was on track to become the NFL's all-time leading rusher. Andre Ware, the 1989 Heisman Trophy winner. Bill Fralic, whom I'd met at an alumni event at Pitt. He was a ferocious blocker and measured 6'5", 280 pounds, and had played in the NFL Pro Bowl four years in a row.

By my count, I was one of 17 quiet and disoriented rookies who didn't even know where our lockers were yet or how to get to the field. We looked like kids compared to the 63 veterans. Eighty players total, the offseason limit set by the NFL. It was the middle of July, the first night of training camp. In about five weeks, 20 of us would be out of a job when the Lions would be required to get their roster down to 60 players. And one week after that, 15 more of us would be back home looking for work when the team needed to get down to the final roster size of 45. After all the cuts during the training camps around the NFL, almost a thousand players would be unemployed.

On the first day of practice, I was standing on the sidelines doing some light stretches when Barry Sanders sauntered toward me. He was the best running back in the league, but I knew that even he had encountered doubters along his path. Because he was only 5'8", he received just one major college scholarship offer from Oklahoma State. But one was all it took.

In his third year in college, he had what is considered the greatest individual season in college football history. He averaged over 200 yards per game. He won the Heisman Trophy in a landslide vote. Astonishingly, some NFL teams had questioned his ability, however, due to his size.

One of Barry's thighs equaled two of mine. His legs looked like he'd stuffed basketballs in his football pants instead of thigh pads.

He looked at me and said, "Hey man. Wanna play catch?"

This became my routine: playing catch with Barry Sanders each day before practice and games. Picking me, a low-profile rookie free agent, as his warmup partner matched his personality. He never craved the spotlight. Barry reluctantly attended the Heisman Trophy presentation via satellite and told people he thought Rodney Peete of USC deserved the award. Barry didn't talk much. He let his playing and work ethic on the field and in the weight room do the talking.

Camp consisted of two practices and several meetings daily. Each day felt like two days. We arrived at the facility around 6:00 a.m. for breakfast. Some players would get taped up or receive treatments from the trainers. I was healthy, so I would join some players in the weight room.

Next, players geared up with helmets, shoulder pads, pants, padded inserts, braces for those in need, and cleats. The first practice lasted from about 8:30 until 11:00 a.m. under the sweltering sun. Then we had lunch and lounged around. Some guys played cards or rolled dice, shouting and laughing. Some slept on couches while many soaked in ice baths. Some read stock market quotes and some read books. A couple of lost-looking

Eight years old, wearing my new Christmas gifts

My parents, Eileen and Tim, after the Gannon vs. Grove City game

My first field goal
as a Pitt Panther.
KELLY CASEY DREHER

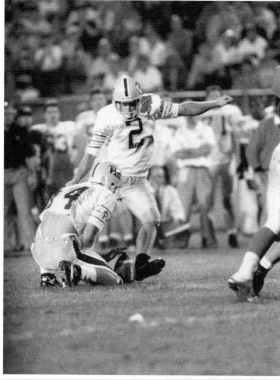

Kicking a 44-yard field
goal against Rutgers
CHARLIE PACK

Meeting fellow captains before the game against Notre Dame, October 1992

During my senior year at Pitt, if I wasn't playing football or with Karen, I was laughing with Andy.

Lions training camp, July 1993

Getting in a pregame stretch with the Detroit Lions

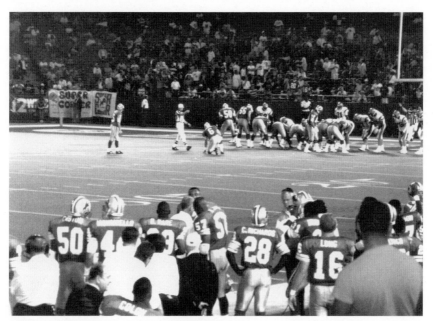

Getting ready to kick "the point after" against the Cincinnati Bengals

In Florida with Karen, February 10, 1994. Next stop, Broward County Courthouse to say "I do."

Karen and Sadie, just a few weeks old, visiting me in Indianapolis

My dad, battling cancer at the time, but happy that I just signed with the New York Jets

Playing for the Scottish Claymores. Not ready to hang up my cleats.

At Amos's house in Pittsburgh, when he was the special teams coach for the Steelers in 2012

Teaching a yoga class at one of our studios, Amazing Yoga

With Karen, Sadie, Summer, Scout, Jack, and Bruiser after playing touch football in the fall

rookies walked around looking like they wanted to cry due to the combination of pain, stress, and uncertainty.

After the short downtime, meetings for the offense and defense began. During camp, players spent more time in meeting rooms than on the field. Then it was time to go back out to the field from 3:00 to 5:00. Some guys sat on the stools in front of their lockers with a look of dread at the idea of putting their shoulder pads and pants back on and taking another beating.

Team dinner in the cafeteria, and then meetings followed the second practice from 7:00 to 9:00. The first meeting was usually special teams, led by special teams coach Frank Gansz. I got to his meeting 10 minutes early; you never wanted to be late for Coach Gansz. Still in tip-top shape in his mid-50s, Gansz had gone to the US Naval Academy and served as an Air Force pilot after graduating. He had 30 years of assistant coaching under his belt including stops at the service academies: Army, Navy, and Air Force. He had built a reputation as one of the best special teams coaches in the NFL. He viewed football as a war game.

On the first day of camp, Gansz had handed out silver Detroit Lion spiral-bound notebooks, and I made sure I brought mine with me to every meeting.

I sat straight up in my seat and watched the players file in. Some limped in with heavy feet and some had their knees or shoulders wrapped in ice. Some had both.

"Open your notebooks, men," Coach Gansz said. "Write this down."

There was a pause. A building of tension. What would today's quote be?

"Those who don't study history are doomed to repeat it," he said as he looked into everyone's eyes one by one. Players hoped not to be embarrassed on the slow-motion film.

With his laser pointer in hand, he then showed a short clip from practice of players missing a tackle on the punt team. He circled the guilty players with his pointer. "Gentlemen, you need to take risks," he continued.

Some players slouched, trying to hide.

"Napoleon once said if the art of war were nothing but the art of not taking risks, then the glory and winning would be in the hands of mediocre talent. Gentlemen, when I was flying my fighter plane in the Air Force, we lived by a creed called *esprit de corps*. Does anyone know what that means?"

A rookie next to me had his eyes closed. I poked him to wake him up so he didn't get caught.

"Sit up straight, men," he said. "*Esprit de corps*. It's the spirit that lifts men above themselves for the good of the group."

The quotes continued throughout training camp. One day while I was kicking, he walked by me and said, "Sean, the body must be energy. The mind directed. The spirit inspired."

I heard him tell a rookie linebacker who was kicking the dirt in frustration as he struggled to pick up a certain technique, "Son, nurture your mind with great thoughts."

And a meeting would never go by when he would forget to tell us, "Men, expect the unexpected."

Once all the meetings were over, there was usually just an hour back at the Holiday Inn to call Karen and watch TV, and then it was lights out. When there was time enough to go back to the hotel during the day, I sometimes caught a ride home from one of the quarterbacks. One day, I hitched a ride with Andre Ware, who was locked in a quarterback battle with three other proven quarterbacks. He was a three-year veteran. I asked him what the hardest part was about playing in the NFL.

"Proving yourself over and over. There's no let up," he said. "It's an endless emotional and physical grind. If you're not performing, someone else will. And you have to stay positive, no matter what anybody says or writes about you."

The more I heard players in the privacy of the locker room and off the field, the more I realized that they were no different from anyone else. Each had his challenges and was trying to navigate through life's ups and downs, just like the rest of us. Guys would complain about the beating of training camp and the pounding on their bodies and minds. Most just wanted to be able to take care of their families and be healthy and happy.

Training camp gave me my first taste of disillusionment with the NFL. I understood why they felt that way as I watched them collide heads with each other day after day.

Each practice, there was a constant crackling of pads and the bump of helmets colliding. Over this boomed the voices of coaches with veins bulging in their necks, yelling like it was boot camp. Some rookies looked like they were going to shit their pants when they were called out for screwing up. Over time, it all became background noise. Players seemed more like drones than people. They'd walk off the field after practice looking like they'd just spent two hours in a washing machine on the spin cycle.

One of the biggest differences between college training camp and the NFL was the constant feeling of tension in the air. The intensity. All business. Jobs were on the line. Players were much larger, more muscular, faster. They were smarter. The ones who had lengthy careers paid attention to the finest details of their technique. They did the small things exceptionally well.

Just a few days into camp, the training room looked like a MASH unit. It was packed with players who had innumerable muscle sprains and strains to their ankles, knees, shoulders, hamstrings, backs, hips, calves, necks, glutes, etc. The coaches wanted to keep the starters fresh and healthy, so it was the new players who would pick up extra reps when injuries happened.

Kevin Colbert made it clear when I saw him early in camp, reminding me of our conversation in which he'd explained that Jason Hanson was their guy and they needed me to take reps when Jason needed a break or in case of injury. But his promise of playing time was more than fair to me. I looked at it as if I was trying out for the entire NFL. I needed game tape. Unless Jason got hurt, I would be let go after the fourth pre-season game. You never root for your competition in camp to get hurt, but you know it could happen. And that thought is always in the back of your mind. Kicker injuries happen too: ankles, hips, groin, quadriceps, low back, and hamstrings.

During camp, I felt like I was on the team, but not. In the NFL, but not. I was on the periphery. And I wanted more than to just make a team. Now that I was closer, I wanted to win a Super Bowl. The ultimate team prize. But first things first.

My first goal was to perform well enough to show that I was capable of being their kicker temporarily in the unlikely event that Jason got hurt during training camp. Goal number two was to get into a preseason game and have video that I could send to teams who were in need of a kicker.

One morning after we had just played the Buffalo Bills in our first preseason game, there was a different guy using the locker next to mine. I asked someone what had happened to the first guy so soon. He said, "Do you know what the NFL stands for?"

I shook my head.

"Not For Long," he said with a chuckle.

According to a recent *Sports Illustrated* article, the average career length in the NFL is just over two and a half years. The NFL requires three years in the league to receive a pension.

Jason, the other kicker, was a three-year vet and an All-Pro. He was clean-cut, smart, and professional, and he shared tips and techniques generously. More than that, he could kick a football a country mile. (Jason retired in 2013 at the age of 42 after achieving an insane NFL record—52 made field goals from 50 yards or longer—and is currently ranked fourth on the NFL's all-time leading scorers list.)

Jason was on his own level. Elite. He was the highest-paid kicker in the NFL, making $750,000 a year, crazy money for a kicker at that time. Today, some of the top kickers rake in around $4 million a year.

I signed with Detroit for the rookie minimum, which was $108,000 per year. But I wouldn't get a dime of that unless I made the team at the end of training camp. In the NFL, contracts are not guaranteed. If you get cut, you don't get any of the money in the contract. (The NFL is different in this way from Major League Baseball and the National Basketball Association, which use *guaranteed* contracts.) During training camp, all players received a per diem. It came to about $500 a week after taxes.

Training camp was six weeks long in the peak of the summer heat, and fighting boredom and monotony was a daily battle. Leisure-time options were limited. I went to see *The Fugitive* at the mall down the street three times. In addition to the perpetual feeling of vulnerability and uncertainty, the other hardest part of training camp was being away from Karen.

To make camp more interesting, the veterans indulged in rookie initiation. Duct tape was a popular tool. One rookie was duct-taped to the goalposts after practice. Another rookie was duct-taped to a chair and placed in the shower while a burly defensive end doused him with alternately scalding and freezing water. No one thought it was funny except the defensive end. A couple of vets who despised hazing rescued the rookie and shot angry glares at the perpetrator, who was laughing alone on his stool.

Possibly because Barry Sanders was my playing-catch buddy, I seemed to be off-limits for radical hazing. Jason, the kicker, didn't care for it, and neither did Jim Arnold, the punter. The worst I had to do was to carry Jim's shoulder pads back to the locker room one day.

After practice one afternoon, a kid wearing a Barry Sanders jersey asked me for my autograph. Surprised yet excited, I signed it. As I walked away, I heard the kid ask his father, "Who was that, dad?"

"I have no idea who number 15 is," the dad said. "I don't think he's anyone important."

I laughed. I was just happy to be there. I didn't want it to end.

• • •

It was about two weeks into training camp and I was watching *Seinfeld* on television. I was on a high. I had just made both my field goal attempts from 43 and 47 yards on a Wednesday night intra-squad scrimmage in the Silverdome.

The phone rang. It was Karen.

"Guess what? I'm coming up to visit!"

I sat up in my bed. "You are? How are you getting here?"

I asked because her Firenza was best suited for traversing short distances from point A to point B in the city. But Karen had decided to push the limits of "point B" to 620 miles round-trip. I reminded her to get a map.

The next day, Karen came rolling into the Holiday Inn parking lot.

She asked for directions along the way from tollbooth workers and gas station employees. Karen wasn't much for maps.

Instead of my usual ride to practice with one of the quarterbacks in a convertible BMW or Mercedes, I got a ride from Karen in her clunker.

The players' parking lot was, as usual, filled with shiny new BMWs, Mercedes, and Acuras. We followed the customary parade of high-end vehicles into the lot and toward the attendant's station; Barry Sanders pulled his light blue Acura through right in front of us. Each player received a nod or a wave from the parking lot attendant.

When we got to the attendant, the one I had seen every day twice a day for about two weeks, I gave him a salute and he fired back with the stop signal.

"Can I help you?" he asked.

"I'm here for practice."

"Practice?" he said. "I'm sorry, but only players can park in this lot. The fans' parking is over there, across the street."

I said, "I'm on the team."

"Show me your parking pass." he said.

I had a program with me from the first preseason game the team played against the Buffalo Bills the previous week. I found my picture and showed it to him. The Firenza was in.

Karen watched practice from the fan section. After my team dinner and meetings, I had just two hours before the mandatory 11:00 p.m. bed check and lights out. We headed to the nearest Applebee's.

Karen brought me up to speed on her life back in Pittsburgh.

"I'm working a lot of hours at C. J.'s. I still haven't been able to get a full-time teaching job. I'm looking for a new apartment; I can't stay in that place any longer, I saw cockroaches the other day."

I went on to tell her how well I was doing, wanting to impress her that I was playing professional football, but she didn't seem to care. She just kept telling me how she was so glad to be with me. The clock was ticking for room check. I'd get fined $500 if I was caught out past curfew.

Back at the Holiday Inn parking lot, we shared a kiss and lost track of time.

"I gotta go. I'll see you after practice tomorrow," I said as I sprinted toward the lobby.

Karen drove away to her home alone for the night, a Red Roof Inn. When the elevator opened on my floor, I heard a familiar chuckle. It was Coach Fontes. I looked down the hallway to the left where my room was. There he was at the end of the hall with two other coaches, laughing with a cigar in his hand. I walked toward my room, straight toward the coaches, hoping I was somehow invisible at that moment.

As I put the key in the door, I heard, "Did you have a good time tonight, Sean?"

Coach Fontes put his arm around me and said, "Because you're out of your room past curfew, I'm going to make you kick a 50-yarder with your left foot after practice." He gave a heartfelt jovial laugh and slapped me on the back.

Karen got back on the highway to Pittsburgh the next morning. The visit felt like a tease, and I only missed her more than before. I gave her a gift before she left: a road map that I got from the hotel. Then I watched her car roll out of the parking lot and disappear down the road. For a brief moment, I was okay with my career uncertainty as long as Karen was part of my life. Then I started to worry about whether she would make it home okay driving her jalopy.

A few days later, they loaded us up into the team bus and we headed to the airport. Destination: London, England. Opponent: America's Team, the Dallas Cowboys, who had beaten the Buffalo Bills 52–17 to become the previous year's Super Bowl champs. Our game was part of the NFL's marketing plan for expanding their popularity in Europe.

Coach Fontes gave us lots of free time, and after a couple of nights of partying, getting up for practice in the morning became a challenge. On the third night out, when I decided to head home early by myself after a few pints, I saw Barry Sanders reading a book in the lobby at 1:00 a.m. He was sitting on a circular marble bench that enclosed a fountain. I was embarrassed to be caught out late by an NFL living legend and hoped he wouldn't see me. He looked up from his book.

"Sean, what's up?" he asked.

He closed his book, and I took a seat next to him. We talked about London and then he asked me about my NFL aspirations. I told him that I didn't want this to end. And I was going to try to find another team to latch on to if Detroit let me go.

"You can definitely play in the NFL. But it's a tough business. So many players, so few jobs. No matter what happens, there's more to life than football."

The game itself was to be held in venerable Wembley Stadium. The aging arena had hosted a range of events including the 1966 World Cup and the Live Aid concert for famine relief in Africa in 1985. The locker room was pure cement, stark and cold, and appeared to be original to the building's 1923 construction, the time of King George V. The field had impeccable grass.

The British "fans" sang haphazardly. They cheered at the wrong times. They appeared confused when the refs announced penalties. Because of their love of soccer and rugby, which gave more emphasis to *kicking* the ball, they cheered louder for extra points and field goals than for touchdowns. The game ended in a lackluster 13–13 tie.

I never made it on the field beyond the warmups. Just two games left before the cut down day. Only two opportunities to get film to keep my career alive.

Our first weekend back in the States, we flew to Texas to play the Houston Oilers in the Astrodome, the world's first domed sports stadium. In the fourth quarter, we held a lead and Jason had already kicked a field goal and three extra points. Frank Gansz shouted at me, "You get the next one. Be ready." My eyes fixated on the scoreboard. I wanted the clock to slow down so I could get in. We never got the ball near the end zone and the clock soon showed all zeros. We won 24–20.

Back in Detroit, we prepared to play our fourth of five preseason games. It was the big cut weekend. It could be my final game. After the game, about 20 of us would be visited by the Turk. Every NFL player on the roster bubble fears the Turk.

The Turk is the guy from personnel who tells you that you've been cut. He could knock on our door at any time during camp. They usually say the same scary eight words: *Coach wants to see you. Bring your playbook.* And with those eight words, it's over. Some players would go to great lengths to avoid the Turk, including hiding under their bed. He was a dream killer. Nobody wants that job.

The day of the game, I was walking through the main coaches' hallway, and as I walked by the head coach's office, I heard, "Hey Sean, come on in. I want to talk with you! Have a seat."

NFL head coaches rarely take the time to talk to a placekicker, much less a rookie placekicker, so I was nervous. Coach Fontes is a big bull of a guy, a former pro defensive back with a barrel chest and a habit of leaning toward you kind of menacingly when he's making a point. But he's also quick with a smile.

I was thinking, *Is this it? It can't be. Just give me one more game.* I heard Coach Gansz's voice in my head. *Expect the unexpected,* it said. Maybe I was about to be cut. The NFL was a business, like Barry said. It was cut-throat. But "cutthroat" didn't fit my perception of Wayne Fontes so far.

Coach Fontes was leaning back in his leather chair smoking one of his signature telephone-pole cigars with his feet up on the desk when he called me into his office. In the previous season, he had taken heat for lighting up a victory cigar on television when the San Francisco 49ers crushed the Bears 52–14 in the final game of the season, which handed the Lions the NFC Central Division title.

"You get in yet?"

It wasn't surprising that he had no idea if I'd seen action in any of the Lions' four preseason games. Head coaches have other coaches to deal with kickers.

"No, Coach."

"Your family coming tonight? Girlfriend?"

"Yeah. They'll be there."

"The girl that you were with past curfew?" he said with a chuckle. "Good. Be ready. Cause I'm putting you in tonight." He blew smoke out of his cigar.

He talked to me like he had known me all my life. He was in no hurry to end the conversation.

"Jason is the best. The absolute best damn kicker in the NFL. And you hung with him in practice. That's something to take with you," he said as he pointed his cigar at me.

After my meeting, I headed down to the locker room. When I walked out onto the field, I spotted my parents and Karen sitting just 12 rows behind our bench in the players' wives' section. I could see her smile 50 yards away when she stood up and waved.

The game was soon underway and I tried to soak it all in, knowing this could be my first and last NFL game. Three quarters went by and I was still a spectator. Should I remind them? No way. This was the NFL; I wasn't going to ask the coach to put me in.

In the fourth quarter, the Lions punched in a touchdown. I saw Coach Fontes looking around. Seeing me, he grabbed the special teams coach, Frank Gansz, and Coach Gansz yelled at me to go in for the extra point.

With no time to warm up, I headed out onto the field. The punter, Jim Arnold, who double dutied as a holder, greeted me. He seemed more excited than I was that I was on the field. Pumped on adrenaline, I split the uprights with a clean kick. Jim smiled and patted the top of my helmet.

As I jogged toward the sideline, I was still in shock that I was actually playing. I had just kicked an extra point. In the NFL.

I felt a single fleeting rush of appreciating how hard I'd worked and what I'd just accomplished. It was just a single point after, but to me, it was a touchdown.

My eyes scanned to the stands looking for my parents and Karen. They were standing and cheering.

But I had to calm down. I took a couple deep breaths and reminded myself there was still a game going on. I had to kick off now.

The coach kept me in for the remainder of the game, and we won the game 30–7.

Shortly after the game, Jim motioned me over to his locker. Before tonight, he had hardly spoken a word to me. "You're a strong kicker," he said. "Someone else is going to give you another shot. You'll make more than that point after."

He shook my hand and slapped my shoulder pads.

Because I knew the inevitable was coming, I was able to say a few other goodbyes to some coaches and players, including Coach Fontes and Barry Sanders.

The Lions released me before the weekend was over. On the whole, it was mission accomplished. I'd performed well in practice and in the final game and got video. Training with Jason pushed me to the next level and I was able to hang in with him almost kick for kick. It built my confidence. The experience would hopefully be enough to get me signed with another team the next season. It was a good start, but I felt like I needed more. It couldn't end already.

CHAPTER 11
SURPRISE PLAY

Karen walked into her apartment and dropped her teaching bag on the floor with a thud. She didn't say a word to me. She sat down on the couch and buried her head in her hands and started to cry. I sat next to her and rubbed her back.

"What happened?"

"I was subbing at Reizenstein Middle School. After school, I was walking to my car in the parking lot and a student yelled at me," Karen sobbed. "He said, 'Miss D, You are lucky you didn't get shot.'"

She explained that she'd been wearing the "wrong colors" on gang turf. Karen owned one blazer: red. This was the last time Karen wore red to school.

She took a lot of abuse as a young sub, and the job could be dangerous. The Pittsburgh city schools were feeling the effects of a national rise in organized violence between the Crips and the Bloods, gangs that originated in Los Angeles. In 1993, 800 people were killed in gang-related violence in LA, and that year marked the highest number of homicides in Pittsburgh due to the gang wars. It was on the local TV stations and in the newspapers every day.

I was now back in Pittsburgh and enrolled in the fall semester at Pitt. I was on the five-and-a-half-year plan and six credits shy of graduating. I moved into an apartment a few blocks away from Karen with a childhood friend and got a job working for Wheel Deliver. People could call in a restaurant order to the office; the office would call the restaurant. Then the office would contact me via radio dispatch: "We need you to pick up some wings and fries at Hotlicks." Off I went decked out in black pants, Nikes, a white shirt, and a bowtie.

My relationship with Karen was strong, but we were both trying to find ourselves. I had my football dream, and Karen was stuck in the world of substituting.

The usually inexhaustible Karen began complaining of being tired every night.

"I think something may be wrong with me. I have no energy," she said.

We both thought it was the stress of teaching in the city schools combined with late nights out together at the bars.

It was November, and the weather was getting cold. My agent, Jimmy, suggested that it might be advantageous for me to move down to Fort Lauderdale near him so I could train while he marketed me to other teams, with the goal of landing me on another NFL roster by next spring.

Sitting on the couch one night, I shared Jimmy's idea with Karen and told her the warmer climate would be better for my back. And that I would only be down there until I signed with a team. As my voice trembled, I told her I thought it was best that I go alone so I could focus on my kicking. My ADD tunnel vision and obsession to make the NFL at all costs put me at risk of losing someone I was madly in love with.

Karen looked at me for a moment in disbelief. After some thought, she replied, "Fine. I'll go live with my friends and get a teaching job in New York while you are in Florida."

What am I doing? Did I really want to risk losing Karen for football?

"What do you think this means for us?" I asked.

"I don't know. Let's just see what happens."

Karen was cool with the unknown. It terrified me.

Losing Karen would hurt more than losing my NFL dream. My heart told me, *don't do this*. But my one-track mind thought this was the *only* way I could get there.

We were both 23 and it seemed like the moves *might* be best for our careers. But it felt like this might signal the beginning of the end of our relationship. I wondered if this was what I really wanted. I began second-guessing my decision.

Over the next couple of weeks, Karen's energy levels dipped to new lows. When she came home one day from work, she couldn't get off the couch. One night while we watched *Seinfeld* together, she wasn't laughing. She suddenly blurted out, "I haven't had my period in a long time."

I almost choked on my nachos.

"You've been late before, though," I said.

Karen was pretty fit, and sometimes her period would be late because of her low body fat.

"I feel different," she said. "Go get a pregnancy test from the drugstore."

I immediately headed over to the Giant Eagle a few blocks away.

In the car, my mind raced. This couldn't be happening. Karen was overreacting. She couldn't be pregnant. We'd only been dating for a year. I was going to the NFL and Karen had her teaching career ahead of her.

I wasn't prepared for all the test options. Pink boxes, blue boxes, multi-pack, single pack, with bold claims like "Number One OB/GYN recommended, results in two minutes," and all touted to be over 99 percent accurate. Since the cheapest one bragged of its accuracy as boldly as the rest, I went for it.

Karen went into the bathroom. Two minutes later, she walked out with the stick in her hand. She showed it to me.

"It's got two dashes," she said.

"Does that mean we're having twins?" I asked.

"It means I'm pregnant," she said.

"Are you sure these things are accurate?"

"How the fuck do I know? I've never used one before."

"I only paid $3 for it. So I bet it's shit," I said. "They had some more expensive ones. I'll go back and buy a couple more."

I approached the pharmacist with a couple of pregnancy tests in my hand.

"Excuse me. Can you tell me how accurate these things are?"

"Oh," she replied. "They're all pretty accurate."

I bought the second most expensive one. It came back positive. I had to read the package insert to confirm what that meant: a *positive* pregnancy test meant you were pregnant. Two for two.

On the third trip to the store, denial was moving toward fear. This was really happening.

I bought the most expensive one they had. It was $18; I put it on my credit card.

After she used it, Karen showed me the stick and she put her hand on the wall to help lower herself to the floor. I sat down beside her. We stared at the empty test boxes and wrappers.

"I don't know what to think," I said. "This wasn't the plan."

"It seems our plans have changed," she replied, and then added, "I'm so scared."

I wrapped my arms around her and held her tight as she cried.

The next morning, with no insurance and no clue what to do, we went to Planned Parenthood in downtown Pittsburgh. The lady we met asked us questions like what kind of jobs we had, how old we were, and so forth. "You both don't seem fit to raise a child right now due to your ages and your career instability," she said. We didn't like that answer, and we didn't understand how she could say that, since she'd just met us five minutes before.

We drove to nearby Schenley Park and found a bench to sit on with a view overlooking the city's skyline. I stared at the bare trees and we didn't say a word for a while. The only sounds were birds chirping and squirrels rustling through the leaves. My mind raced. I knew I wanted kids someday, but how was I going to be a good dad if I was supposed to be giving it all to be in the NFL?"

"I'm so ashamed of myself," Karen said. "I'm terrified to call my parents. What will they think?"

I looked out at the clouds surrounding the downtown buildings.

"Maybe we should call Father Larry," I said. Karen had never met Father Larry, but I'd told her stories about how he had helped me in the past, back when I called him Deacon Larry.

"Father Larry, when was the last time you spoke with him?" Karen asked.

"I don't know. It's been a few years. But he will tell us what to do."

"Will he be mad at us? We're Catholic."

"He's a priest, he's not allowed to be mad at us," I kidded.

We drove back to Karen's apartment and called Father Larry. Karen grabbed the phone in her bedroom while I used the one in the kitchen.

"Hey pagan, where the heck have you been?"

"I want you to meet Karen, my girlfriend. She's on the other line."

I caught him up with the situation. We thought he would judge us.

"Everything is going to be okay," he said. "And you're going to make great parents," he said.

I figured he was just doing his job, being kind and saying all the right things because he's a priest.

"As soon as we hang up, go up to Erie and tell your parents. After you visit your parents, stop over and see me. And one other thing: get married," he continued.

It was comforting to know that we had at least one person who appeared to not judge us. But we still felt overwhelmed and uncertain.

That weekend, we drove to Erie and shared the news with our parents. We worried about what they would think. Even though we'd known each other since high school, we'd been dating for only a year. We did love each other; we knew that. They each took the news expressionless. Like us, they had to go through the shock first. But they handled it much better than we thought, and showed far more confidence in us than we'd guessed they would.

On the drive back to Pittsburgh, I told Karen, "I'm glad our parents and Father Larry believe in us, but I bet our friends will think we won't last."

"Could you blame them?" she said. "We're a statistic in the making." After a moment, she said, "You still need to go to Florida."

"What do you mean? We're going to have a baby in eight months," I said.

"You need to pursue your dream. You don't want to ever look back and think that you didn't give it your all."

"And what about you and New York?" I asked.

"I'm going to move back home with my mom for a few months. Do what you've got to do in Florida and I'll come down as soon as I feel ready. I just need some time with my mom. I have no idea what I'm doing. I've never been pregnant before."

And I think she needed some time away from me. I felt self-centered and selfish. But Karen knew how my obsessive mind worked. She told me to concentrate on kicking and she would focus on having the baby. She was okay to put her teaching career on hold and she would figure out what was next after she had the baby.

If she had asked me to stay, I would have, but she started to exude this air of confidence that everything would be okay. There was no protesting.

The following weekend, I graduated from Pitt.

It was late December, and snow covered the ground; about a week remained before I'd be leaving for Florida. I hoped to propose to Karen before I left, though I doubted I could afford to buy her a diamond ring. I talked to my dad every day. He rarely told me what to do, especially now that I was "grown up." He was a professional listener. When I told him my plan to propose, he responded with a straightforward, "That's good."

Father Larry, on the other hand, quite enjoyed telling me what to do. When I told him that I wanted to propose, he responded, in his mild Pittsburgh accent, "My aunt works at a jewelry store at the Clark Building on Liberty Ave. I'll call her today and ask her to get you the cheapest price possible. Go downtown and see her tomorrow morning, and she'll take care of you."

I scrounged together every dollar I had. I managed to come up with about $200 from my restaurant delivery job. Before I left the apartment, I checked the mail. There was a plain white envelope postmarked Erie, Pennsylvania. A white piece of paper unfolded to reveal five $20 bills. The note read: "Put toward Karen's ring. From Dad."

When I arrived, Father Larry's aunt greeted me warmly and asked me how much money I was looking to spend.

"Three hundred dollars," I said.

How about size? Then she schooled me on the three Cs.

"Can you just show me what you think are the three best ones for $300?"

She showed me three different rings, all priced more than $300, but said that I was getting "the Father Larry deal." They were all beautiful gold rings with the tiniest diamonds, but I didn't think it would matter to Karen. I picked one.

Three nights before I left for Florida, I took Karen out to the scene of our first date a year before, Max & Erma's.

She ordered her usual black bean rollups and I got the buffalo chicken sandwich with bleu cheese. We had the bar all to ourselves. The bartender watched the hockey game on the TV at the other end of the bar.

After I took my first sip of beer, Karen looked at me, her cheeks glowing. "You're going to propose to me, aren't you?" she said with a throaty laugh.

"Why do you have to ask that? You're blowing the surprise." I fiddled in my pocket for the ring, feeling tongue-tied.

"Surprise? We're at Max & Erma's, the site of our first date, and I'm pregnant. And you have that look on your face."

"Why can't you just go along with it and act surprised?" I cleared my throat. "Will you—"

"Yes, of course I will marry you!" she said before I could finish asking, with a smile the size of the sun. She planted a hard kiss.

"Don't you want to see the ring?" I asked.

She put it on and gave me a hug.

Everything seemed to be moving so fast. *How's this all going to work out*, I wondered. I felt fear and excitement simultaneously.

We didn't set a wedding date or anything like that. It was more like, "Let's get married eventually, 'cause we probably should."

I still had a surprise for her, however. To escape from our roommates, I had booked a room at the Hampton Inn out in the suburbs. For $59, we got an indoor pool, cable TV, hot tub, newspaper, and an all-you-can-eat continental breakfast.

We didn't sleep much. We were the first ones at the continental breakfast and we sat alone and talked.

"How do you feel about being a dad?" Karen asked.

"It doesn't seem real yet to me," I replied. "But I'm going to train even harder now to make the NFL. We're going to be a family." Then I added, "Are you okay, if I keep trying to make the NFL a little while longer?"

Karen nodded. "You have to keep following your dream. And I'm coming along for the adventure." She grabbed my hands on the table. "This is all going to work out."

A few days later, I was on Interstate 95 South heading to Florida to see Jimmy, my rookie agent.

• • •

My blue 1983 Honda Civic had over 120,000 miles on it, but it still drove smooth. I stuffed the car with my belongings, placed my ball bag in the trunk, and southward I went on New Year's Day for the 1,270-mile trek from Erie to Sunrise, a new suburb right outside Fort Lauderdale. It seemed like a logical plan in my mind. I would drive to Florida, move in with my agent for a couple of weeks, then find my own place, while also finding a job. Karen could meet me by March. I would train in the beautiful sunny weather, my agent would land me a new gig on an NFL roster, and we'd be out of there by May and live happily ever after.

Jimmy greeted me with a big hug. He had a place for me in a guest room near the kitchen, but it soon became clear that nobody else in his household wanted me there.

I tried to keep as low a profile as possible. In the mornings, I grabbed a quick breakfast and engaged in small talk with his wife. Her first question each day was, "Did you find a place yet?" His teenage daughter didn't speak to me. She gave me the stink eye. I couldn't blame her.

At night, from my tiny spartan room, I'd hear Jimmy's wife asking him how much longer I was going to be there and asking him why he's always taking in these *lost* kids.

The clock was ticking. Each day, I hit the pavement hard looking for a place with a cheap, short-term lease and a job that would pay a decent wage and allow me time during the day to kick and lift. My only friends were the voices on my cassette tapes: Snoop Dogg, Axl Rose, and Steven Tyler. On the third day of driving around, the water temperature guage in my car went into the "H," as in hot. I replaced the coolant and water in the tank, hoping my car just needed assistance in the transition from the frozen tundra of the North to the hot and humid South.

The next morning, Jimmy took me out for breakfast. Jimmy seemed like he was the mayor of Sunrise. Everyone knew him. "Jimmy!" the guy from behind the counter shouted as we walked in.

He was dressed in a blue Nike tracksuit and his hair was slicked. After breakfast, he was headed off to the gym to coach basketball where he worked with at-risk teens.

Absent this morning was his usual warm smile. He fidgeted with his gold watch while we looked over the menu.

"Sean, I'm really sorry, but you have to move out . . . today. I know I said you could stay with me for as long as it took you to find a place and a job, but my wife is just not down with it."

It turned out Jimmy had never actually told her I was coming. He'd known she would say no, and was just hoping she would change her mind when I got there. I didn't know anyone in Florida I could crash with. How had I gone from NFL player to homeless in no time flat?

Desperate, I drove over to a strip of dirt-cheap hotels in the Hollywood section of Fort Lauderdale, where I got a room for $20 a night. Not exactly the Ritz, but it did include mystery stains on the bedsheets and a toilet that ran all the time to keep me company. It also came with prostitutes who knocked on the door all night offering their services and the added bonus of full access to the drug dealers who lived up and down the halls. At night, I heard fighting and screaming and knocks on the door, with occasional gunshots off in the distance.

On my second night, at three in the morning, there was a loud knock on my door, much different from the soft knocks of the prostitutes. The knock was followed by an angry voice: "Hey you in there! Get out here. I'm going to kill you! Hey Randy, you owe me money, motherfucker!"

Who the hell was Randy? I didn't own a cellphone yet, and my room had come without a phone. I decided to wait it out, and after 30 more minutes of relentless yelling, Randy's "friend" gave up and left. I packed my bags, and when the sun came up around 6:00, my ass was out of there.

I grabbed the Fort Lauderdale newspaper at a grocery store. At this point, I had already called at least 20 apartments with no luck. In the apartment ads, something jumped out at me: "2-bedroom apartment in Coral Springs. $400 a month shared with female roommate." A female roommate—what would Karen think? I called, and a woman named Tammy told me to come over at 5:00.

I hit the pavement looking for a job. As I was driving down Highway 1, my gauge started approaching hot again. I called Jimmy from a pay phone at a gas station and he said to meet him at his friend's garage in Plantation in an hour. When I pulled into the garage, five guys swarmed the car and started poking around the engine.

"$3,000," one of them said.

"Your car is worthless," said another.

I asked Jimmy if these guys were pulling my leg. I missed my dad's friend who owned a repair shop in Erie, who'd never jerked us around. We stretched cars for years. But Jimmy said they were telling the truth. I still felt like I was getting screwed. I didn't have $3,000 to fix this car and I sure as hell didn't have money to buy a new one.

No car. Now what?

Jimmy gave me a lift in his BMW to a Honda dealership, where his friend was the manager. The man offered to lease me a new Honda Civic for $200 a month.

"Lease?" I said. "My credit sucks."

"Do you think your dad would sign a loan for you?" he asked.

"I need some time to think about this," I said.

I walked outside with Jimmy and asked him what he thought.

"Don't worry about the car payments. You'll be back in the NFL and you'll be able to trade it in for a BMW," Jimmy said.

I stared back at him. This didn't smell right.

"Your other option is to park it in a shitty neighborhood and leave the keys in the ignition. That's what I do when I want to get a new Beemer."

I called my dad. I told him how great things were going. I left out the drug dealers, the prostitutes, and potentially moving in with a girl not named Karen. I just said I needed some wheels. My conservative father was not an impulsive decision maker.

"They want you to get a lease?" He said it with fire in his voice. After a few minutes, Jimmy asked if he could talk to my dad and smooth talked him. My dad was still queasy but he agreed to sign. I promised to pay him back every cent of the deposit. An hour later, I was driving out in a brand-new navy-blue Honda Civic. Next stop, Tammy's apartment.

I drove west over Royal Palm Boulevard into the 20-year-old planned community of Coral Springs, which contained no actual springs. It was 20,000 acres, once beautiful marshland right next to the Florida Everglades. Developers had drained it and built a city of apartment buildings and strip malls as far as the eye could see.

A friendly redhead in her early 30s with an Ohio accent showed me the two-bedroom apartment, then interrogated the crap out of me for 30 minutes to make sure I was on the up and up. "I want you to know I have a boyfriend," she said. "I want to be clear that there won't be any funny stuff."

I explained I had a girlfriend too, who was coming to visit next month. Then I used her phone to make a quick call to Karen.

"Good news. I have a new car and a new apartment," I said. "The only thing is . . . I'm sharing the apartment with a girl."

"You're joking, right? I'm stuck up in Erie right now with three feet of snow. I'm pregnant. I'm fat and tired. And you're hanging in the sunshine living with a strange girl."

"It's totally cool. You'll see when you get down here."

"When I hang up, I'm calling USAir and booking my flight," she said.

I moved in that night.

The next day, I hit the streets again in search of a job. In the trunk of my car was my bag of balls, four of them, one tee, a pair of cleats, and my trusty homemade ball holder. It went with me everywhere I went. Whenever I had some spare time and saw an empty field with goalposts, I'd pull over and kick some balls.

While I was kicking every day in Florida, Karen was doing downward dogs in Erie with a beginner yoga VHS tape. Karen told me months later that sitting at home all day as her body grew and changed and strange hormones coursed through her system, she became trapped in her mind. She felt large, lethargic, and moody. Clothes didn't fit. She had no job. She felt lonely. She had no friends nearby and her mom worked all day. She told me how her self-esteem plummeted. She imagined her friends having fun in New York City with their new jobs while she was alone reading *What to Expect When You're Expecting*. There was nothing in the how-to manual that mentioned her present scenario of being 23 and having a boyfriend with no steady income seven states away.

One lucky day, I stopped by the Palm-Aire Resort in Pompano Beach. It was an expansive resort built in the 1950s near the Pompano racetrack, and it attracted all kinds of interesting guests, including Elizabeth Taylor and Jerry Lewis. At one time, Billie Jean King was the tennis pro.

I scored a job as a bellman. I made a little bit more than minimum wage and received tips from the guests. It was going to be just enough to allow me to scrape by.

The job had some unexpected perks. The New York Yankees stayed there during training camp. One of my duties was to deliver the dry cleaning each morning to the Yankees owner, George Steinbrenner. He always answered the door in his boxers. He'd open the door halfway, hand me five bucks, and grunt, "Thanks, kid."

One day, I drove some guests to a strip joint after they'd finished their round of golf. On the way back, the radio broadcaster announced a bulletin: "Today, a 6-foot-tall, 200-pound man wielding a police baton charged up to Olympic ice skater Nancy Kerrigan and clubbed her on her knee."

At the resort, I said to the other bellmen, "Did you guys hear what happened to Nancy Kerrigan?"

"Yeah, crazy," one said. "But even crazier, Frank Sinatra just checked in and he's down at the bar."

"No way," I said.

"Don't believe me? Go down to the lounge. He's there with all his bodyguards."

I strolled down to the lounge. There he was, drinking what appeared to be whiskey on ice, surrounded by some tough-looking dudes.

He had a couple of bodyguards who looked like extras from *Goodfellas*. They sat outside his room and shared stories with me each time I saw them. At the end of their stay, they gave me a brown bag with a half-drunk bottle of Jack Daniel's and a six-pack inside. "This is for you kid. Mr. Sinatra drank from the bottle."

One night, I returned home to lights flashing on my voice mail. I hit play. My Pitt football buddy John's voice trumpeted out: "Hey Cons, it's

John. I'm coming down to Florida tomorrow. I'm bringing down a mattress and I'll just sleep on your floor. I'll help you train and hold footballs for you. I'll call you sometime tomorrow on my way down to get the address."

He had to be kidding. I knew he'd been trying to get a job as a police officer; I guessed it hadn't worked out. The next morning, I called his parents. His dad answered, and I asked for John.

"John? He left early this morning. Said he's on his way to Florida."

I told Tammy about our potential third roommate, and she said, "No problem, as long as he helps out with rent."

The next day at 2:00 p.m., John knocked on the door.

"How did you get here so quick?"

"I drove the whole way nonstop, Pittsburgh to Florida. Sixteen hours."

"That's impossible!"

"No it's not," he laughed. "I only stopped for gas. I just peed in a cup and tossed it out the window as I was driving."

John got a job waiting tables at a popular restaurant in Sunrise, one frequented by supermodels and real estate hotshots. The stage was now set for Karen's arrival. I was living with a girl, and John would be sleeping on the floor while Karen, who was expecting in six months, would be jammed into the twin bed with me.

In February, on the day of Karen's arrival, I met her at the gate and watched her walk out with a huge smile on her face and a beautiful bump in her belly. When I'd left in January, she wasn't showing, and the reality of the pregnancy struck me in a whole new way.

Driving back to Coral Springs, I thought it might be wise to mention the slight change of circumstance.

"Hey, um, John is here too now," I said.

"You mean John Bruner from Pitt?"

"Yeah, he actually moved into the apartment."

Karen stared at me. "Where is everyone going to sleep?" she asked.

"He just sleeps on the floor, next to our bed. He brought down his own mattress."

While John and I worked night shifts, Karen and Tammy would sit in the living room and talk. Tammy enjoyed the arrangement and especially Karen's company. She would drink Miller Lites and vent about her ex-boyfriend while Karen sat listening. During the day, Karen kept herself busy by hanging out at the community pool reading *What to Expect When You're Expecting* and tagging along with me when I went to kick. She'd walk around the track while I practiced and get in a few yoga poses whenever she could.

• • •

"Let's get married down here," Karen said one afternoon as we were sitting by the apartment pool. She was wearing her white, sporty, one-piece maternity swimsuit with an anchor on it.

"Isn't that called eloping? What about the big Catholic wedding we're supposed to have? What will our parents think? What about Father Larry?" I asked.

"They'll just be happy we're getting married. We can have another wedding in Erie later."

"All right," I said. "Let's do this. How about the chapel at Disney World? I'll call and see how much it is."

A five-minute phone call determined that Mickey Mouse and Donald Duck were way out of our budget.

"I bet you a million bucks Jimmy has a *friend* that would marry us. I'll give him a call," I said.

I was right. Jimmy responded with a big belly laugh. "A friend? I can do better than that. My brother Larry is a judge in Broward County. He'll do it for you for free."

"What's the catch?" I asked.

"You just have to put up with him for an hour," he replied.

Next on the to-do list, wedding rings. Driving to work one day, I noticed a giant outdoor flea market. The Florida Swap Shop had an indoor and outdoor flea market, amusement rides, a video arcade, and drive-in movies. One of the dozens of vendors had a sign that read "Exchange Cash for Gold." Jackpot. The next day, Karen and I went to the flea market, and $30 later we had our wedding rings.

We counted up our money and figured we had just enough to go to the Florida Keys for one night after we got married in Fort Lauderdale. It would be our honeymoon.

The following week, we parked in downtown Fort Lauderdale, then entered the Broward County Courthouse building and took an elevator to meet the judge. Larry turned out to be a spirited character and quite the talker. A former Bronx taxicab driver, he would later gain notoriety for being the presiding judge in the Anna Nicole Smith case.

After some quick pleasantries with me, he gave Karen a kiss and a hug that lasted a little longer than I was comfortable with. Our witness for the "ceremony" was his receptionist, a bleach blonde with implanted breasts popping out of her skintight shirt, who needed an extra 10 minutes to put on some makeup. Halfway through the short ceremony, the judge paused and jokingly (I think) asked Karen: "Why are you marrying a loser like him when you could drive to South Beach with me in my cool red convertible?"

Karen responded with an uneasy laugh and looked at me like, "Can we get this over with?"

Fifteen minutes later, it was official.

The world was ours now. We were penniless, but in love and on an adventure. Everything would go our way now we thought.

After the ceremony, we made a quick lunch stop overlooking the ocean in South Beach to people-watch the Rollerbladers, muscle heads lathered in baby oil, and European topless sunbathers, then headed off to Key West. We soon discovered that Key West was much farther than it looked on our *Rand McNally Road Atlas*. With the sky turning black and stars beginning to appear, we stopped in Key Largo for dinner.

As we sat at our table getting ready to order, a woman two tables over had a massive heart attack. The paramedics took her away.

"I think she may be dead," Karen said. "Maybe we should go home."

We did a quick money check. As much as we wanted to have some sort of romantic stay in Key West and visit Ernest Hemingway's house, the money wasn't going to stretch far enough. We left the restaurant before ordering. We pit stopped at Arby's and got five roast beef sandwiches for $5. Wedded bliss.

• • •

In the meantime, the offseason was coming to a close, and I was running out of time to find a spot on a roster. Jimmy lined up a one-day workout/tryout with the Dolphins, who were just a half hour away in Davie in a pristine, state-of-the-art training facility dotted with towering palm trees.

I wasn't concerned about my accuracy. As usual, my concern was my kickoffs, which were getting spotty due to my ever-growing back pain. I was going to a chiropractor once a week by that point, and I scheduled a session the day before the workout in hopes of healing my mysterious imbalance. I popped a few Advils and a Flexeril on the car ride over just in case I got a spasm. I had my fingers crossed that we'd do kickoffs first, when my leg was fresh, and field goals second.

The special teams coach, Mike Westhoff, took me, John, and Jimmy on a tour of the facilities. Upon entering the training room, we were greeted by the sight of Dan Marino completely full-frontal butt-ass naked. He was getting out of some sort of ice treatment for a torn Achilles tendon he'd suffered the previous season while playing the Cleveland Browns. I had an ally. I thought of the time I saw him and his colorful and inspiring words he passed along to me in the bar near the Pitt campus.

As we walked onto the field, which smelled of a fresh cut, Westhoff said, "We're looking to sign a kicker who can kick the ball into the end zone. We'll start with 20 field goals and end with 10 to 12 kickoffs. Let's see what you got."

The workout began well; my kicks were even clearing the enormous fence behind the goalposts. Some of them hit the side of a van parked in the lot, smack dab in the center behind the goalposts. I figured it had to belong to one of the players. Each time I hit the van, Coach Westhoff let out a cackle.

"Should I back up so I don't keep hitting that van? I might be denting it," I said.

"Nah, I know whose it is. He won't mind," Westhoff responded with a smirk.

I kicked another one over the fence and it hit with the loudest thud yet. At the same time, the training room door opened and out limped a man with his foot heavily wrapped. Dan Marino, all 6 feet 4 inches of him, walked straight toward the van.

Of course.

He leaned over and stuck his face next to the door to inspect it. We stopped and stared. I held the ball under my arm, anticipating the humiliation of being yelled at by Dan Marino. Westhoff and the ball boys laughed under their breath. The moment was 10 seconds, but it seemed like an hour. Finally, he stood up and looked back at us.

"Let's see if you can do it again!" he shouted at me.

My next kick hit his van dead on again. And then again.

"Westhoff! Sign that fucking kid up right now," Marino shouted.

"Let's move on to kickoffs," Westhoff said.

The ball boy placed five balls on the 30 yard line. I grabbed the ball closest to me and gave it a few squeezes. It's a last-second ritual many kickers perform to make the ball softer and rounder. The balls appeared brand new, but they would have to do.

New footballs (made by Wilson Sporting Goods, the same company that makes the volleyball Tom Hanks talks to in the movie *Castaway*) are hard, unforgiving, and skinny, which gives them a smaller sweet spot than a broken-in ball. New balls are still coated with a film that makes them slippery. They don't travel as far as worn-in balls.

Kickers go to extreme lengths to doctor up their balls before games. It is an art. One way to get a ball with a bigger sweet spot was to fill the ball with as much air as possible until it looked like a rugby ball and then throw it into a clothes dryer and watch it bang around. Once the ball was nice and toasty, you'd brush it down with a horsehair brush. Some kickers would push the noses of the balls into a table and then put them in a sauna for two days. Others would bake their balls or even microwave them. One guy used to soak his balls in lemon juice and evaporated milk. All legal at the time. A dirty little secret.

Today, the balls can still be wiped, rubbed, and brushed, but must be inspected by the referees and marked with a special "K" and subbed in on kicks. Kickers throughout the league complained, but statistically nothing changed much.

Out on the field with Westhoff, I took my usual approach. I placed the ball on the one-inch-high red tee, standing it almost perpendicular with a slight lean back toward me. Laces out. I turned around and jogged back 10 yards at a slight angle and turned around to face the ball. I stared at the ball perched on the tee, and then glanced downfield at the goal line. It was 70 yards away. One of the ball boys was standing in the grass of the end zone, where the word *DOLPHINS* was drawn out in white chalk letters. I looked at the kid and imagined kicking the ball over his head.

I approached with a slow jog for the first five yards and accelerated for the last few steps. My left foot planted firmly in the short grass and I felt my foot strike the ball with a powerful punch. The impact and stroke carried my body a few yards past the tee. It felt good. I looked up, and the ball was soaring end over end. I glanced at the ball boy. While looking up to catch the ball, he was *backing up* from the goal line. He caught the ball four or five yards deep in the end zone. *Yes!*

Four or five more kicks like that, and I'm back in the NFL, I thought. But the next kick felt different. As the ball flew through the air, the ball boy took a few steps to his right and then . . . a few steps *forward*. He caught the ball on the goal line. Five yards shorter than the first kick. Still pretty good, but I wanted better.

The next kick, the ball boy caught it on the 2 yard line. Coach Westhoff, who wouldn't stop talking during the field goal session, went eerily silent. I could feel his disappointment. My body felt smaller. I kicked five more kickoffs, and only one found the end zone. The other four landed between the goal line and the 5 yard line.

The difference between kicking the ball to the 2 yard line or into the end zone is the difference between a job and the unemployment line. Everything is black and white. Just like field goals, make it or miss it. For kickoffs, you kick it into the end zone or you don't. Coming *close* won't get me on the team.

My performance was not quite NFL material, and I knew it.

After the workout, Coach Westhoff gave me and Jimmy his assessment. "You have the best lift I've seen with the exception of Chip Lohmiller," he said, referring to the kicker for the Washington Redskins. "That ball comes off your foot high and fast. Even the tallest linemen are never going to block your kick."

Coach Westhoff continued, "You have great accuracy on field goals too. But, I'm concerned with your kickoffs. It doesn't make sense to me;

your field goals are traveling at least sixty yards each time. But when you kick off, they don't get any further. I'm not sure if it's a technique issue or what it is."

He was confused because kickoffs should be easier than field goals. Kickers line up for a field goal just three yards away from the holder. The ball is placed on the ground, leaving a kicker's feet to battle the grass.

For a kickoff, kickers go as far back as 10 yards, and the ball is placed on a tee. The ref gives the kicker 25 seconds to kick the ball. This creates a setup with less pressure. Science, physics, mechanics, and logic would dictate that a kickoff should go farther, yet mine did not.

I knew exactly what the problem was. My back and leg were wearing out.

"We're not going to sign you," Coach Westhoff concluded. "I need a kicker who can consistently put their kickoffs into the end zone."

I said hateful words to myself as I tossed my cleats and other gear into my ball bag.

That was it. It was April, and my bold move to Florida had resulted in nothing except further damage to my leg. As John drove me back to Coral Springs in total silence, the sky turned dark and it started to rain.

When I came home to the apartment, I dropped my bag on the floor.

"It didn't go well?" Karen asked.

"It was going great until my fucking leg gave way at the end."

After I gave Karen more of a recap, she said to me, "You take drugs every day and spend all this money going to the chiropractor. It's not healing your back. When we go back to Pittsburgh, you're doing yoga with me."

CHAPTER 12
BLINDSIDED

"Time to open your body and center your mind," said the man on the TV. He was shirtless in skintight black shorts and sporting a long ponytail.

"I'm not doing this!" I said.

"You made a deal," Karen reminded me.

I'd agreed to do yoga with her once a week. Karen was six months pregnant and she didn't complain, she just did the yoga. We were watching a video with Rodney Yee, who asked me to turn my senses inward. I didn't know how that could help me land an NFL gig.

"Give it a chance," Karen said.

I resisted it, but I knew better than to back out of a deal with Karen.

I landed a temporary job as a UPS driver. It was April, and I was at the end of my rope. If I couldn't sign with a team by May, when teams had usually completed their rosters for summer training camp, my career would be over.

My desperate situation led to desperate ideas. One night, sitting on our deck overlooking the movie theater from our perch on the hill, I sipped a few Honey Brown Ales. An idea popped into my head.

"What if I put on my UPS uniform and went down to the Steelers' practice facility on my lunch break saying I had a delivery? I'll ask Coach Cowher if I could have another workout," I said.

Karen said, "That's awesome."

But the next morning, without the beer muscles, I came to my senses.

I decided it was best to let Jimmy go. The relationship between players and agents is "at-will" and I didn't owe him anything since I wasn't on an active roster. He had done all he could. He pleaded to keep working for me, but he understood I needed a fresh approach. Jimmy would later become a successful high school head basketball coach, winning the Florida state title in 2015.

I decided to be my own agent. I dug up the worn-out sheet of paper, now as soft as tissue paper, which contained the name and number of every NFL team. I photocopied it to give it new life, and I started dialing away. But after making calls to all the teams, I came up empty-handed. No one seemed interested.

But then, three days later, on a Monday afternoon, I was slipping on my brown work uniform when Coach Tom Batta, the special teams coach for the Indianapolis Colts, called to invite me for a workout on Wednesday. He said they'd be working out another kicker, and I'd have to pay for my own lodging and transportation. This meant I was the "throw-in guy," the guy they were less interested in, but it didn't matter. It was an opportunity, and that's all I wanted. Besides, when I kicked side by side with another kicker in a competition, I always stepped up my game.

Karen walked into our basement apartment around midnight after waitressing for eight hours down the hill at Sullivan's Restaurant.

"I'm driving to Indianapolis tomorrow," I said. "Do you want to come?"

"Yes! Of course!" Karen screamed.

On Tuesday, Karen (who was now seven months pregnant) and I set off on the six-hour drive due west on Interstate 70. The next morning, after getting more than my money's worth from the free continental breakfast, I felt pretty good, so I decided to skip my usual horse-pill-sized ibuprofen and Flexeril tablet.

When we arrived at the Colts' training complex, the receptionist invited Karen to wait in the lobby area and escorted me to the field, where I met Coach Batta and the other kicker. We engaged in awkward small talk, exchanging names and where we played college ball. We sized each other up like George Foreman and Muhammad Ali before a title bout. He was a carbon copy of me physically: at least 6 feet tall and a solid 200 pounds. He probably had a strong leg, and if the Colts had brought him in, he was good.

Coach Batta told us we had 20 minutes to warm up. After a short jog, five minutes of stretching, and a few minutes of light kicking, I was ready. I was getting smarter and knew to save my energy. I was laser focused that day. *We're having a baby in two months, I don't have a job, and I feel good. Let's get this started.*

As the other kicker kept stretching, I told Coach Batta I was ready. I could get it over with and then let him kick while I went off to the side. I didn't want to watch the other kicker because his performance didn't matter. All I could control was what I did, and at the end of the tryout, it would either be good enough for a contract or it wouldn't. Simple as that.

I started with 30-yard field goals. After the third kick, I'd back up five yards. Soon I was back at 45 yards, my favorite part of the field, where I felt most confident, knowing I could show off my strength. I wasn't going to miss today. I was having fun. It was like I was 12 years old again, kicking balls on the dirt field near my house. I was feeling, not thinking.

My adrenaline raced as I drilled all three. Each kick would have been good from 60 yards, sailing as high as the top of the uprights.

I went back to 55 yards. I made all three. I was on.

But I knew kickoffs were next. I begged my leg to hang on.

The kicking gods were with me that day. All 10 kickoffs found the end zone. Coach Batta nodded as he looked on.

It was my best workout yet in front of an NFL team. When the other kicker went, I stood in the corner of the field with an equipment manager and made small talk, pretending to watch but looking mostly at the clouds and thinking about what Coach Batta thought.

At the end of the workout, Coach Batta walked us off the field and told me to wait while he spoke with the other kicker in the lobby. I waited on the turf field and shot the shit with the ball boys. I was also playing psychologist in my head, wondering whether meeting second was a good or bad sign.

One of the equipment managers came out and told me that Coach Batta was ready to see me. I walked into the lobby, where I found Coach Batta and some other Colt employees all talking to Karen. She was the center of attention, receiving midwestern hospitality because of her beautiful baby bump.

"Can you hang around for a while?" Coach Batta asked.

"Absolutely," I said.

He headed back into the office and returned five minutes later with some paper in his hand.

"The Colts would like to compensate you for your travel and hotel expenses," he said, and handed me a check. It was $300.

Coach Batta talked to us for about half an hour. He asked about the baby and about coaches and players we knew in common. His parting words were, "We'll be in touch." We left feeling good, but in the NFL, there were no certainties.

Back at home, my mind was racing as I drove around town on my delivery job. I'd be listening to sports radio but all I could think was, *When will they call? Will they call?* A lot could happen in a few days. Another kicker they found more attractive could become available. Perhaps a trade. Or maybe they were just being nice because Karen was pregnant.

A week later, I walked into the apartment and was greeted by a flashing light indicating two messages on the answering machine. I sprinted across the room, stumbled over the coffee table, and hit play.

"Hi Sean, it's your mom . . ."

Beep.

"Sean, Coach Batta. Give me a call. I'll be in the office until six tonight."

I scribbled his number down on the back of one of Karen's *Cosmopolitan* magazines, and then I called him back.

"We want to sign you to a two-year contract," he said. "The workout wasn't even close. You were the easy choice."

I was back in the NFL.

The Colts asked me to come early on July 10 with the rookies, about five days before the veterans. This meant more kicking—and possible training fatigue. I'd worry about that later. The Colts' kicker was 32 and had had an up-and-down career to that point. If I kicked to my ability through training camp, my chances were good at winning the job.

But wait. I had somewhere I needed to be on July 10.

When I told Karen the news, she was ecstatic. But she soon came to the same realization that I had: "I'm due on July 10!" After a pause, she said with bright, mischievous eyes, "I wonder if there's a way to make a baby come out before the due date."

Since I couldn't ask the Colts to let me stay with Karen until we had the baby, she consulted her OB/GYN, who said, "To get things moving, I'm prescribing you lots of sex and exercise."

Karen started working out three times a day. She taught kickboxing. Hit the treadmill. Yoga and tangling in the sheets at night. Repeat.

On Wednesday, June 29, 1994, I had 11 days until training camp, 11 days until the baby arrived. We'd decided to name the baby Callahan, if it was a boy, or Sadie, if we had a girl, after Karen's grandma, whom I'd never met. She'd died when Karen was 10 years old, and Karen had had a special relationship with her.

My mom called and told us, "We're going to Cedar Point for a couple of days. Don't have a baby while we're away."

Off they went, with my brother and sister, driving four hours to Cedar Point Amusement Park in Sandusky, Ohio, to ride rollercoasters and eat funnel cakes.

Like most Americans at that time, we were glued to the television watching the latest updates on O. J. Simpson. We were watching the trial and they were grilling some surfer-looking guy named Kato Kaelin when Karen put her hands on her belly. "I'm getting contractions."

This was it. We packed her bags and got in the car.

I pressed on the gas as Karen hid her face in her hands.

I hit 85 miles an hour on the highway screaming toward downtown Pittsburgh. We weaved our way into the parking lot of Magee-Women's Hospital. Once we got back to see the doctor, she measured Karen's dilation and said she was less than two centimeters.

"You're not going to have the baby tonight. Go home. When the time between your contractions is three to five minutes and they last longer than 30 seconds, come back."

"Are they serious?" I said.

It was midnight when we got back in the car. We rolled into bed and slept lightly.

Around 5:00 a.m., Karen started moving and got out of bed.

After a couple of minutes, I heard Karen yell from the shower, "Oh my God!"

I walked in to find her doubled over and moaning.

She got out of the shower and waddled straight to the toilet, almost slipping.

She threw up.

We started timing. They were five minutes apart, on the money, and lasted 30 seconds apiece.

We hopped back into our Honda for round two. Karen sat with her hands on her belly and the seat reclined and said, "The baby is going to come out now!"

"No it's not!" I stepped on the gas and waved at the slow cars in front of me to move out of the way.

As soon as we made it into her hospital room, her water broke.

• • •

On June 30, 1994, at 1:23 p.m., Karen gave one more push, and Sadie made her first appearance. All nine pounds, nine ounces, and 23 inches of her. They laid Sadie on Karen's chest. The look in Karen's eyes was euphoric.

"She's so beautiful," she said.

My body felt as if I'd taken a huge exhale, now that Karen was no longer in pain and Sadie was safe and sound. Everyone was healthy. They'd made it.

In this moment, my NFL dreams were pushed out of the picture.

After a few minutes, Karen said, "It's your turn to hold her."

I'd never held a baby before. She looked so fragile. I wasn't even sure how to pick her up, she was so tiny.

She had the most heavenly scent. I looked in her eyes and told her that I loved her and I never wanted to let her go. I began to cry. I kissed her on her soft pink cheek.

It was the greatest day of my life. When we brought Sadie home, I spent hours holding her and staring at her. Something happened to me in those moments—a shift way more significant than anything I'd ever encountered. It was like my code was being rewritten. I looked back at my life up until that point and all I saw was how self-absorbed I had been. All the time, it was me, me, and me.

I saw how I had attached every ounce of my self-esteem and identity to being a professional football player, and I'd made my happiness contingent on achieving my goals. *I'll be happy*, I had always assumed, *when I've become a stable NFL football player*. Now I had an inkling that maybe happiness originated somewhere else entirely. Could it be that I'd find it not in my achievements, but in my ability to love? On the eve of my big chance with the Colts, my perspective began to change radically. What if, I thought, "making it" in the NFL wasn't the sole purpose of my life? What if it wasn't the only route to joy? Sadie's birth started to shift everything about my world.

I was a father. For the first time, I began to think that it would be okay if my dream ended tomorrow. The moments I spent with Sadie and Karen in the 10 days before I left for training camp outweighed any moment on the football field. It felt liberating.

As I drove along the flat highways to Indiana, my mind bounced around, and the pressure of making the team began weighing on me again. I was a *father*. My dream couldn't be about me anymore. Now more than ever, I needed a career in the NFL to take care of and provide for my daughter.

•••

The camp was held in Anderson, Indiana, a small town an hour northeast of Indianapolis, on the tree-filled campus of Anderson University. I was assigned a dorm room with a nervous rookie safety from Montana State for a roommate.

I met the team's current kicker, Dean Biasucci, who looked like a movie star. It turned out he was an actor on the side; after his retirement, he would go on to get an acting gig portraying himself in *Jerry Maguire*. Dean had been in the league for 10 years, and, like I said, he'd had some up-and-down years, which meant the position was "open" for competition. Up for grabs. My job: unseat the proven NFL veteran.

But to win the job, I'd have to outperform him convincingly. A huge advantage of being a veteran is that you've already proven your mettle in real games. I had no such experience. A cruel truth of the professional football business is that the system pits players against each other, and you might end up hoping the other guy struggles during camp so you look better. I tried not to fall into this poisonous trap and to focus only on what I could control: my own kicking.

But competing for the job was awkward. It was an unspoken reality, me versus him. In Detroit, it had been clear there was no competition. This was different. For the Colts' management, it was advantageous if I won the job. If Dean kept his spot, he'd be paid his annual salary of $700,000. I signed a two-year contract for the league minimum, so I would be paid $108,000 if I were named the kicker at the end of camp and $135,000 if I made the team the following season. The team saw me as a $600,000 annual savings. Plus, I was just 24 and had what they thought was a fresh leg.

Camp started well. My field goals were sharp and my leg powerful, just like the workout in the spring. I felt comfortable and connected with my holder, the quarterback, Jim Harbaugh, who was new to the team like me. He too had signed with the Colts in April. He'd spent the previous seven years with the Chicago Bears.

Jim was always moving. Always talking. Some guys on the team considered him kooky and intense, but I found his love of the game to be infectious.

Jim was an amazing holder—a skill that's harder than it looks. The holder kneels on the spot where the ball will be kicked, usually seven or eight yards behind the line of scrimmage (where the ball is hiked). The kicker uses his right foot to mark where he wants the holder to place his pointer finger. The kicker then steps away from the spot. The holder looks back at the kicker. When the kicker is ready, he gives the holder a nod. The holder raises his arm and the ball is snapped back almost instantaneously. The ball sometimes comes into his hand with the laces facing the kicker (which can cause some kickers to panic seeing the strings and think, *O shit, that's not how I kick*), in which case the holder must spin the ball to correct it so the laces face out. He must then tilt the ball at the exact angle preferred by the kicker. The kicker then must do his job by hitting that tiny sweet spot. All this must happen in 1.2 seconds. Any more and the kick is most likely blocked by the sprinters coming from the ends diving with their long arms outstretched. Quicker means you are rushing and likely to get sloppy.

When all this happens in unison, kickers make it look easy.

After wrapping up a morning kicking session a couple of days into the second week, Jim patted me on the helmet and told me, "Keep doing what you're doing." I was already feeling confident, but being supported by a veteran quarterback didn't hurt.

After that morning's practice and a shower, I walked alone along the campus path toward the dining hall. Walking along an adjacent path about to intersect with mine was the head coach, Ted Marchibroda.

"Let's grab lunch together, Sean," he said.

The head coach knew my name. Good sign. Wanted to have lunch with me? Great sign.

We small-talked as we stood in line with our trays in hand. I loaded up with spaghetti, beans, rice, Gatorade, and extra bananas to take back to my room. We took seats across from one another among the crowd of starving giants chowing down.

"I grew up not too far from you," he said.

He was from Franklin, a tiny Pennsylvania oil boomtown almost smack dab in the middle between Pittsburgh and Erie. He told me about his fond memories of playing quarterback for the Steelers in the 1950s, including a year off while he served in the Army during the Korean War before returning and rejoining the team.

Marchibroda was an innovator. While coaching the Buffalo Bills in the 1980s, he was known for using a no-huddle, "hurry-up" offense throughout an entire game. His offensive strategies helped the Bills go to four straight Super Bowls.

"You've caught the coaching staff's attention in practice," he said. "Keep it up. You have a chance to make this team."

My throat constricted and my heart surged. I could practically taste it. I urged myself to keep calm and prayed my leg wouldn't fail me now.

About two weeks into camp, my rookie roommate from Montana was getting homesick, nervous, and defeated. Every night, lying in bed with his voice muffled, he'd call his girlfriend and talk to her for at least an hour and complain about everything: the food, how hard it was, the coaches, the heat. Tonight, he was ready to throw in the towel.

"I don't think I can last through training camp," he said. "The NFL's not fun."

"Stay positive," I told him. "Just another few weeks."

I could relate. Despite my focus, my stomach felt ill during the downtime, as I was missing Karen and Sadie.

Since I'd left for training camp, Karen had been staying in Erie with her mom. She would send me care packages about once a week. One box contained a diaper with fake poop in it to remind me what I was missing. Karen spent the hot summer days learning on the job.

I knew she was having a hard time of it, but when we talked, Karen was so positive, telling me, "You're going to make the team."

• • •

Our first preseason game was against the Seattle Seahawks at home. It had been almost a whole month since I had seen Karen and Sadie. Karen called me a few days before to tell me the great news that she was thinking of hitching a ride with my parents and bringing Sadie, who was just four weeks old.

In the dome, right after the national anthem finished, I saw them squirm through the crowd looking flustered and wiggle into their seats. Karen explained to me later why they had been late. As they'd approached the exit for the Indianapolis Hoosier Dome, my dad drove past the turnoff twice.

We won the game 13–9, but I didn't see any field time and was told by Coach Batta that my chance could come the next week.

I showered and changed as fast as I could. I was the first player out of the locker room. When I walked out, they were all there waiting for me in the sea of players' families, girlfriends, and wives. Karen was holding Sadie. After kissing and hugging everyone, I took Sadie from Karen's arms and held her tight.

I talked fast, as I could see the bus loading up. I wanted time to stop. I wasn't ready to go back to the dorm. But before I knew it, almost all the players' families had dispersed and the bus was almost full.

"I have to go. You guys should head back too, it's dark now."

I kissed Karen and Sadie one more time and hugged my parents goodbye before I hustled to the bus. In my seat, I looked out the window and watched them walk toward their car. I felt like I was leaving my heart in that parking lot.

The following week, the two sessions per day began to take their toll on my body. I had to find a way to keep my strength up. But the only way to do that was rest, and rest wasn't an option. I woke up Tuesday morning and my lower body felt stiff as a board. It was as if someone had stuck a knife in my lower back. I felt 84, not 24. I lay motionless, staring at the ceiling, pleading with the football gods not to let this happen today.

Using my hands to support my weight, I crawled like a baby over to my dresser. I reached for my stash of Flexeril and horse-pill ibuprofens. I dug out the Advils and took four, totaling 800 milligrams. I recalled a trainer once saying that was the maximum safe dosage for the liver. I figured there was a margin of safety, so I swallowed one more, putting me up to 1,000 milligrams. Without water, I swallowed them whole. Then I took a full Flexeril; I didn't care if I got groggy. I felt like the Tin Man.

I couldn't go see the trainers and tell them I was injured. That would be the kiss of death for a new guy. If you're not already on the team and you get injured, you have little to no value to them. Damaged goods. It would have to be my secret.

Over the next couple of days, the pills helped mask the pain, but they didn't give me more strength. I started to fatigue early in practice. And even with the pills, I felt intense pain in my hip flexors and down the sides of my legs. The pain began to manifest in my head as well. When I looked at the ball on the kicking tee, instead of appearing elevated (it was two inches off the ground), it began to look low, and the sweet spot looked smaller. The goalposts looked farther away. The end zone seemed to be a country mile away. My leg felt heavy, like I had sand in my pants.

Dean sat out some of the practice sessions and rested. As a veteran, he'd earned this option. He had already proven himself. He could only *lose* the job, but he didn't have to try to win it. On the days when Dean didn't kick, I was kicking 30 to 40 balls. I then remembered that Gary Anderson from the Steelers had told me how he took the whole summer off. I began to get pissed at myself. If only I had trained *less* all these years, maybe I wouldn't be in this position of weakness. I would be an established kicker in the NFL. But now, rest was out of the question. Deal with the pain. Just like all NFL players do.

I was asked to take the bulk of the kicks each day, and as the new guy, I had to keep kicking. From the sidelines, Dean saw my leg strength dwindling. He could see his competition knock itself out of contention.

I didn't take Dean's tactic personally. I might have done the same if I were in his shoes. Dean had a family to support; sometimes, he brought his two-year-old daughter along to practice. Watching him play tag with her around the trees made me daydream of Sadie.

My options were clear. I could keep my mouth shut and continue to go along with taking the bulk of the kicks. That would surely expose my weakening leg, and then I would undoubtedly be cut. Or *what if* I went to Coach Batta and explained to him that I needed some rest—and just hope he'd grant me a breather without thinking I was soft. As I let these options battle it out in my head for a few days, the pain increased, and my kick distance shortened.

I picked up the phone and almost dialed Amos's number to ask for his advice. But I didn't, because I knew what he would say. He'd taught me to be straight with coaches. *Be honest with your coach and tell him what's going on.* I could practically hear his voice in my head, and I listened. I had more to lose by saying nothing.

Before practice that morning, I went to Coach Batta's office. First, I did a walk-by in the hallway. I felt sick to my stomach. Admitting weakness was against everything I believed in at the time, and I was terrified he was going to think I was a wuss. It's the NFL. Macho men only.

"Good morning, Coach," I said, walking into his office.

"What's going on?" he asked.

"Coach, my leg is really tired and it could use some rest. Would you consider letting me take a session or two off?"

He sprung from behind his desk and walked toward me as I stood just a few feet inside his doorway.

"You're a new guy who needs to come in here and show what you can do. Get ready to kick today. Suck it up."

I apologized for asking what now looked like a stupid question. Even though I sensed a disaster in the making, I didn't begrudge Coach Batta. This is how most coaches thought at the time, and how many still feel today. Besides, it was I who'd been obsessed with kicking hundreds of balls in the offseason, I who had fatigued my leg in the first place. I was just now figuring out that *less could be more* sometimes, but it wasn't the coach's fault that I'd worn myself down before I learned that lesson.

The morning's practice was open to the fans and they lined the perimeter of the field. Late in the session, they called out, "Field goals!" *Stay alive,* I thought. *Get through this.*

Dean stood on the sidelines with his helmet off, in a front-row seat for the horror show that was about to begin.

The coach had us line up from the 28 yard line, which meant a 45-yard field goal attempt, my favorite.

But today, the goalposts looked a mile away and as narrow as railroad tracks.

I lined up to kick and Harbaugh set the ball down and spun the laces out. I hit it as cleanly and as sharply as I could. The ball left my foot with a whimper. As soon as I kicked it, I knew where it was going. I knew without looking up that this one did not have the power needed. I looked up and saw the ball fluttering and struggling to make it to the goalposts. It trickled just over the crossbar. I hadn't kicked a ball that short since I was 15.

Being in an NFL camp was where I had always wanted to be. But right now, I wanted to be anywhere else.

I had two more chances to kick from 45 yards. Both were an exact replay of the first kick. My leg felt detached. My heart shrank.

The air horn blew to signify the end of practice and possibly the end of my career as a Colt.

In addition to the fans, the whole team, the coaching staff, the general manager, the trainers, and even the owner were there that day, watching.

Pro sports is an unusual profession in that your performance is so public. A rough day at work broadcast for the entire world to judge and see.

I didn't want it to end this way. I didn't want to look at anyone. I felt naked, on display.

I pictured Karen at home taking care of Sadie and imagined her feeling the disappointment of learning that I'd missed out on my best chance yet to make the NFL.

I'd blown it.

I stood on the sideline by myself as practice shifted to a new session. No one said a word to me, with the exception of Jim, who put his arm around me and asked, "Hey, are you okay? Are you hurt? You should go see the trainer."

I had a horrible feeling that this would be the last time I would work with Jim. He knew my performance was crushing me inside. As I walked away, he told me, "You have to have a short memory. You have to forget about it."

I went to the training room, and when no one was looking, I grabbed a few ice packs. After the evening practice, I grabbed a couple more. Hopefully, my self-treatment would go unnoticed.

"The fucking Turk is coming for me," I told my roommate.

"Maybe he will cut both of us," he said. He couldn't wait until the Turk knocked on our door for him.

Lying in bed, I prayed for more time, a second chance, a miraculous healing of my back and hip or whatever was wrong. In five days, we would be flying to Pittsburgh to play the Steelers. My family would be there, and my friends. It was a homecoming. I desperately hoped I could at least make it to the Steelers game.

The night passed with no visit from the Turk.

The next day after lunch, instead of my usual nap, I just stared at the ceiling.

Deep in the back of my mind, I knew my career would be finite. But I always tried to keep that thought buried. *What if* I get cut. *What if* I don't have what it takes to make the NFL?

It was around 2:00 p.m., a couple of hours before we'd hit the field again.

Then came the knock.

I pretended not to hear it.

The Turk. The grim reaper.

The guy was someone from the scouting department whom I recognized but didn't know by name. He had a somber look on his face, like a funeral director.

"Conley, grab your playbook. Coach Marchibroda wants to see you."

He turned around and left.

I walked down the stairs from my second-floor dorm room and crossed the burnt grass lawn to the coaches' offices. Coach Marchibroda's office door was half open. He was sitting at his desk with a sad look on his face.

"Come on in, Sean." His eyes lacked their usual sparkle of enthusiasm. "This wasn't an easy decision for us," he said.

"You started really strong at the beginning of training camp and we hoped you could push Dean. You looked like you ran out of gas on the field. Keep your head up. You have an NFL leg."

He stood up from behind his desk and shook my hand, looked me in the eye and wished me luck. I thanked him for the courtesy and the opportunity. A Colt employee who was standing outside the door walked me down to another office. Walking papers. He slid a piece of paper in front of me and told me to sign. I didn't read it. I didn't care what it said. I was in a trance and just wanted to sign it and escape.

I took the long way back to the dorm to avoid running into other players or coaches. I didn't want to talk to anyone. Especially Coach Batta. I ran into one of the ball boys and he said, "See you at practice."

I grabbed most of my clothes and gear and stuffed them into my duffel bag. Forget about my razors, toothbrush, even my clothes on the ground. While I packed, my roommate told me he was jealous. I could hear other guys getting ready for practice. I wanted to sneak out without them seeing my face so I wouldn't have to explain that I had just been cut.

With my box fan in one hand and my duffel bag over my shoulder, I walked straight to my car. I tossed my stuff into the trunk and exited the campus. I parked my car in a fast-food restaurant parking lot just outside the school's main gate.

I could see the yellow goalposts and the stadium lights. I rolled down the window to get a clearer view. I sat in the parking lot for a while, thinking about what had happened, and how I had given everything of myself to my goal. Where would I go from here? What was I going to say to Karen? What was I going to tell my parents?

I got out of the car and pulled my calling card out of my pocket; it had a few dollars left on it. Inside the phone booth, I picked up the receiver to call Karen and then decided I just wanted to get out of there.

I took the back roads. Route 36 East to Route 22 into Pittsburgh. While driving through the country roads of Indiana, I shouted at myself. I thought of the old saying that the definition of insanity was doing the same thing over and over again and expecting a different result. My over-training and perfection quest had been insane. And now, it had cost me a once-in-a-lifetime opportunity to break into the NFL.

I didn't think I would get another shot after getting cut a second time. Most players don't ever get a second shot. To get a third chance would be beating impossible odds. It felt like the final blow.

What would I do without the camaraderie of teammates, the physical challenge, and the natural high of playing? Without the NFL, I didn't really know who to be anymore. How could I be a good husband and father? Football had become part of me.

After a few hours, I stopped to fuel up. I called Karen. I got the answering machine.

"I got cut. I'll be home in a few hours. I love you."

When I pulled into the apartment complex parking lot, I sat gripping the wheel for a few minutes. I walked into the apartment and Karen leaped from the couch. We hugged each other tight.

That night, she and I talked over cheap wine.

"This may have been the best chance I ever get to make the NFL," I said. "I'm so pissed at myself for blowing it."

"You didn't blow it. But you can't keep kicking yourself over it," Karen responded.

"I planned to get everyone tickets for the Colts and Steelers game this weekend. I'm so embarrassed," I said.

"Embarrassed? Because you got cut by an NFL team?"

The sight of Sadie sleeping in her crib shook me momentarily from my frustration. She was so much bigger.

I wasn't going to give up. I had come too close. But this one really hurt.

On Thursday night, the night before the game, we went to Houlihan's, a bar downtown with an outside patio. We were on our second beers when Karen said, "Those guys over there are looking at you. Do you know them? They look like football players."

It was a half-dozen Indianapolis Colts, all friends I'd made at training camp, mostly rookies and second-year guys. There were a couple of linebackers, defensive backs, and a couple of wide receivers. I tried hiding behind a group of happy hour drinkers.

But one of them spotted me. They walked over and gave me man hugs. One said he envied me: "You're lucky you get to just watch now and don't have to put up with two-a-days." I wasn't sure if I should believe him. However, many players acknowledge that despite all the glory that can come with it, the NFL is, at heart, just a business. One that destroys their bodies and minds. Bill Parcells, the Hall of Fame coach, said what players wanted deep down was "to keep their jobs, make their money, and go home."

After an hour or so, it was curfew time. We hugged, slapped hands, and I wished them all good luck. I watched them walk out of the patio bar. *That should be me.* I took a big chug of my beer as they headed up the steps.

"It's just you and me now," I said to Karen.

CHAPTER 13
ICING THE KICKER

The next few weeks, I drove an ice cream truck to pay the rent. The music system played the same happy tunes over and over, while my mind just replayed the same gloomy memories. That last moment on the field in Indianapolis. Everyone watching as I failed. The Turk knocking on my door. I felt powerless to stop it.

I landed a better-paying job working for College Credit Card, soliciting students to sign up for credit cards. The job entailed stuffing our car as full as possible with free handouts like Twizzlers and T-shirts. Students would receive giant Kit Kats for filling out a one-page credit application. For every application filled out, I got a dollar.

Surrounded by candy bars and T-shirts, we squeezed in Sadie and her car seat, though I couldn't see out the rear window. We'd set up our table of goodies in the school's student center. I would stand behind the table and Karen would hold Sadie to help sales, as a baby was a college student magnet.

I'd take the ball bag given to me by the Detroit Lions and find a spot for it among the hundreds of T-shirts. Then I'd find fields at the college campuses and sneak on.

As we traveled around the country, we'd hole up in hotels on the weekends and watch the NFL on TV all snuggled together on the queen bed.

I felt angry and useless watching other kickers. There is an old saying, comparison is the thief of joy. I was my own thief; I couldn't stop stealing my own joy. While watching games, I couldn't shut my mind off. *Why did*

I over-train so much? I'd think. I'd try to remind myself that I was a father first, and a football player second.

At bedtime, I'd hold Sadie and lay her down in bed and smile. In those moments, I'd remember that there was more to life than football. But as soon as I was alone, my mind would get busy again.

The NFL season ended on January 29, 1995, with the San Francisco 49ers destroying the San Diego Chargers 49–26 in Miami. And it was time again to start bothering special teams coaches.

I wasn't done. I was an NFL kicker.

I came up with a new game plan. More rest. Less kicking.

After all the rejections, however, I felt I needed a new voice to call teams. I had spoken to every NFL special teams coach and player personnel guy multiple times. I even knew some of their secretaries on a first-name basis. So I gave John a call to brainstorm.

"I want to give it one more shot. Any ideas for an agent?" I asked.

"Yeah, me."

John had just gotten a part-time job as a policeman in Hanover, a rural area about an hour south of Pittsburgh.

"I charge 0 percent."

After I hung up, Karen, who was eavesdropping on my conversation, couldn't contain her enthusiasm.

"I want to try this, too!" she said.

The three of us started making calls. We were the Three Stooges Pro Sports Agency. John put all the names and numbers into what he called his "agent pad," a two-by-four-inch pocket journal.

One afternoon, Karen walked into our basement apartment in suburban Pittsburgh. I was holding Sadie, feeding her a bottle. She'd just taught a kickboxing class at the gym, and she was drenched in sweat, her brown hair pulled back into a bun.

"Any luck today?" she asked.

It was March of 1995. Snow still lay in dirty piles on the roads of Pittsburgh. Five weeks had passed since Super Bowl XXIX. The team list was covered with red-and-blue ink, a layered patchwork of scattered notes such as "don't call back" and "not interested."

"I have just two 'we'll think about its' from the Steelers and the Jets. Everyone else has said no. I talked to Pat Kirwan, the player personnel guy for the Jets. He seemed interested."

But a couple of weeks went by and the Jets still hadn't called back. The car was loaded up, ready for our drive to Maryland the next morning for College Credit Card. We were about to leave when the phone rang. It was Pat Kirwan, inviting me to come up to New York for a tryout.

I nearly pulled the phone out of the wall with excitement. I looked over at Karen and gave a thumbs-up and she jumped up and down with her hand over her mouth.

As the plane descended toward New York City, from my window seat, I saw the magnificent skyline. I felt as if I were so close to finally getting to the top, just like the buildings soaring into the clouds. There were 28 teams in the NFL. The 28 best kickers in the country, the world, solar system, the universe. Right now, I was ranked somewhere between 29 and 40. I was so close to breaking through.

The next day, my confidence was high. The Jets had a kicker, Nick Lowery, who was almost 40, whom they were looking to replace.

Waiting for me was the special teams coach, Ken Rose. Coach Rose had just retired from an eight-year NFL career one year prior, playing for the Eagles and the Jets. He still was built like a linebacker.

For tryout time, he assembled a crew of assistants to track the number of field goals I made, the distance of my field goals, and the hang time on my kickoffs.

My eyes surveyed the field. The Jets building complex. This is my future.

I'd been here before. Pumped on adrenaline, I nailed my first four from 40 yards. Every one sailed easily in. I was in the zone.

"Okay, I've seen enough from here," said the coach. "Let's move back to 45 for the next two."

I made both with ease.

"Let's move back to 50."

After I made the first five in a row with room to spare, he said, "Damn! This is unbelievable. I've never seen anything like this. You need a challenge. Let's move back to 60 now."

I was feeling, not thinking. Not trying so hard.

The ball boy put four balls down on the 50 yard line. When you add in the 10 yards for the end zone, it makes it a 60-yard kick. I figured if I could make at least two, I'd have a job again.

I took my three steps back and step and a half to the right. I gazed down at the goalposts 60 yards away. They looked close: a good sign. I gave the nod to the holder that I was ready. The center whizzed the ball back; the holder placed the ball down and spun the laces forward. I hit the ball with a clean strike. I glanced up and the ball was soaring end over end toward the goalposts. Good. Right down the middle with room to spare. I looked down to hide a grin.

I was operating on instinct, flow, and determination. It all seemed so simple, just strike the ball just right and it will fly.

The next kick was a carbon copy of the first.

Kick three was wide right by just a few feet.

Kick four snuck into the right-hand corner.

Three out of four.

We finished the workout with kickoffs, all of which found the end zone.

I'm going to be a New York Jet, I thought.

"That's one of the most impressive workouts I've ever seen," the coach said.

I felt like hugging him.

"I'm going to go talk to Pat Kirwan and see if he wants to meet with you."

About 10 minutes later, Coach Rose came back and walked me to Kirwan's office. He would have the final say in signing a player. He all but told me they'd be offering me a contract. "We'll call you the day after the draft." He told me they wanted me to be their "man," and wanted me to come in and unseat their current kicker that fall.

I left New York without signing a contract, but it seemed imminent. They dropped me off at the airport and I headed for the nearest pay phone to call Karen.

"I think I'm a Jet!"

Karen had dreamed of moving to New York City ever since her college days at Fordham. It was like a dream come true.

The 1995 NFL Draft concluded on Sunday, April 23. On Tuesday, at around 5:00 p.m., Pat Kirwan called, saying, "We'd like to bring you into camp and sign you to a two-year contract." I threw my baseball hat into the air.

But there was little time to celebrate. I still had to earn my spot on the team during mini-camp, a three-day camp, which started in about a week, and then in training camp, beginning in August.

It was late April, and I had a week to get ready for mini-camp. I wanted to kick every day, but I was a little smarter now. I kicked just twice and just a dozen or so balls each time. I stretched, had the chiropractor adjust my spine, lifted just a couple of times, and prayed that my injury wouldn't rear its ugly head for three days in May.

At mini-camp, they gave me a green-and-white Jets jersey, helmet, shorts, and shirts and assigned me a locker across from quarterbacks Bubby Brister and Boomer Esiason. On day one, Coach Rose said, "No team kicking today on the schedule. Just kick on your own."

I watched practice from the sidelines with the punters and the other kicker, Nick Lowery. The quarterbacks, wearing red mesh jerseys to make them stand out, barked signals: "Blue forty! Red ninety! Set-*hut*!" I just soaked it in and watched them zip spirals around the field. They made it look so easy.

On the second day, I kicked a half-dozen 40-yard field goals with the team. I made them all. Nick watched from the sideline.

On the final day of mini-camp, the weather changed. A strong wind was blowing toward one end of the field. Kicking into the wind is a kicker's nightmare. It was going to knock at least 10 yards off field goals and kickoffs in that direction.

"Let's do some kickoffs," Coach Rose said.

In seconds, he orchestrated the kickoff and kickoff-return teams. The kickoff team would be facing the fierce wind. *Shit.*

"I'm going to sit this out," Nick said to Coach Rose.

I'd seen this movie before in Indianapolis. I knew what the incumbent was doing. The veteran trick of the trade.

I picked up a few blades of grass and let them go. The wind carried them a few yards before they fluttered to the ground. A headwind. For a moment, I considered requesting we kick in the other direction. But if I did, I'd look like a baby. I'd kicked into the wind hundreds of times. Anyway, I felt great mentally and my leg felt strong.

I placed the ball, then jogged back eight yards and faced the ball standing up on the red rubber tee. The wind howled through my helmet's earholes. I waited a moment to see if the wind would die down. It didn't. I told myself to do exactly what I always did. *Don't try to kill the ball. Don't mess with my mechanics.* If I tried to kick it harder, I'd risk missing the sweet spot, which could change the rotation of the ball, and the wind would knock it down quicker.

My first kickoff flew high, though the rotation slowed as it fought the wind. It landed near the goal line, which was excellent given the conditions.

"The next two, kick them deep to the left," he shouted.

Both kicks soared high and deep in the left-hand corner of the field. *Don't let up.*

"Down the middle."

On the next kick, as I struck the ball, I felt a shooting pain up the front of my leg at the top of my hip. I winced in pain.

I looked down the field. The ball fluttered sideways through the air and bounced around the 20 yard line.

Keep going. Kick through the pain. You've done it before.

On my next kick, when my foot connected with the ball, I felt very little force. Like my leg was saying, *All done.* The ball floundered through the air low and bounced on the grass around the 15 yard line. My right quadriceps had gone on total engine shutdown.

Two bad kickoffs in a row. I had to make up for it on the next one. I walked back eight yards. The wind intensified. I waited, but it seemed like it was only getting fiercer. My leg was dead and I was kicking into a gale. I couldn't wait any longer. I approached the ball, and my mechanics came completely unglued. I tried crushing the ball, and felt a jolt of pain in my hip again. The ball squibbed and bounced down the field haphazardly.

After practice, I sat staring into my locker. If I did and said nothing, they'd certainly cut me after my performance. I had nothing to lose. If I went to their team doctor, he might find I had a minor injury, and then hopefully, the Jets would be patient and allow me to heal—without terminating my employment.

As I walked down the hall to see the team doctor, searing pain traveled up and down the outsides of my legs. At age 25, I felt old. Defeated.

I went into the physician's room and told him my history: low back pain, hip flexor pain, leg muscle weakness. He had me sit on the table with my knees bent and dangling over the side, then push my thighs up into his hands, one leg at a time. When he asked me to do it with the right leg, it felt as if I had no strength. His hand was too strong, and I couldn't budge it.

He began to manually examine my hip flexors. He dug into the left, and everything seemed fine after just a few seconds of poking around. He then examined my right side. The hip flexors are at the very top of each thigh, where they connect to the hip. They connect the leg, abdomen, and pelvis. Hip flexor tightness affects posture and causes back pain. Our hip flexors help us with all our basic movements: lifting our knees, climbing stairs, bending over, and even walking. They are some of the most powerful muscles in our body.

A few seconds of searching on the right turned into a minute.

"I'm having a hard time finding your right hip flexor muscle," he said, baffled.

My heart sank. I felt sick.

"I'm afraid," he said, "that your hip flexor muscle has degenerated from overuse."

I pretended not to hear him.

I pictured my thigh muscles torn to shreds. I stopped breathing.

"Will I be able to play football again?" I asked.

"I wouldn't advise it."

"Isn't there some rehab I can do or something?"

He just looked at me and shook his head.

A *kicker* who couldn't kick. It couldn't end like this.

I flew back to Pittsburgh. For seven days, I waited. And then, finally, it came.

I recognized the area code on the caller ID. I could have let it go to the answering machine. But I answered.

Pat Kirwan told me how I had the talent to play in the NFL and other complimentary stuff. But the conversation ended the same.

"I'm sorry, Sean, but we need to release you."

CHAPTER 14
GAME OVER

After the initial trauma of being released, reality set in. I needed a job. I called teams in the World League of American Football.

I refused to accept the physician's prognosis. Maybe with even more rest and stretching, I would have a spontaneous miracle healing. Maybe another NFL team will notice me if I play in an alternative league. Don't give up.

It was a start-up league in Europe funded by the NFL with rosters made up of current NFL players who needed more seasoning and former NFL players trying to get back to the NFL. The league had teams in six cities: London, Barcelona, Frankfurt, Dusseldorf, Amsterdam, and Edinburgh.

In mid-May, the Scottish Claymores' head coach, Jim Criner, returned my call. They were five games into a 10-game season. They had a sudden opening for a kicker. It paid $1,000 a week to play the game I love.

He asked me if I could get on a plane the next day and meet them for their game in Germany.

I flew to Frankfurt on the next flight available. Karen was still on board for the adventure. "I'll come visit!"

I checked into the hotel and waited for the team to arrive the next day. After a nap, I walked the cobblestone streets and tiny alleyways. The next morning, the team bus pulled up. Coach Criner came in and met me in the lobby. All eyes locked on me as I came into the bus. A moment of anxiety. I found the nearest empty seat next to a tall lanky quarterback.

He reached out his hand. "You must be Sean Conley the kicker," he said. "So glad you are here. We need you."

I was on a team again.

After the game, I found myself in Scotland; we were staying a few miles north of a castle nestled on the North Sea. Ancient stone farms dotted the countryside. My first practice with the team, the temperature was in the 40s and there was a swirling wind. Cold and dreary. The grass in the rugby stadium was emerald green and the sky was filled with clouds upon clouds. Welcome to Scotland in June.

Guys stood on the sidelines slouched over in their long, royal-blue raincoats with their hands in their pants.

"I just wanna go home," one of the players said.

The team was dreary like the weather, but I found beauty in it. I was still alive. I didn't want it to end. I wanted to go out on my own terms. I wanted a chance to savor it all, take it all in.

I asked myself *what if*, over and over. I couldn't give up my identity as an athlete. It made me tough and confident.

While watching practice, walking along the North Sea, I felt like someone bouncing through time. The past. Anger. Frustration. What could have been. What I could have done. The future, if I were to heal and get fixed. The present. The beauty of Scotland. I wondered how other people let go.

At practice, I pictured my hip flexor. Was it just a thread of muscle barely hanging on, like the Jets' team doctor had said? But I could walk, run, and kick. I kept taking my muscle relaxants and lots of Advil. My heart ached leaving behind Karen and Sadie, but I was excited to bring home some money, presents, and hope again for an NFL job.

Our last game was in London. I made two field goals and finished the season having made nine field goals. In the locker room, Coach Criner told me I'd earned a bonus—$2,500, my biggest paycheck yet—for having the second-highest field goal percentage in the league. My six weeks in Europe were over.

But when I came home in the middle of June, the phone remained silent. No NFL team called. I knew I would have to face this reality eventually, but it was a reality I never wanted to accept.

I went back to my delivery job. Karen was teaching spinning and kickboxing and waitressing a couple of nights a week. An old friend asked her to take at-risk teens into Algonquin National Park in Ontario, Canada, for a few weeks.

Sadie was now two years old, a little person. She could talk, dress herself, and feed herself, and even had her own little potty to sit on.

I thought of the last resort, the Arena Football League. It was an indoor league made up of teams like the Iowa Barnstormers and the Miami Hooters. It paid $500 a week. The number of players that had gone from the AFL to the NFL was miniscule.

I looked at the list of teams and their phone numbers. Instead of accepting that my football career was over, I picked up the phone and started dialing. Instead of trusting my intuition and hanging up my cleats, I talked myself into doing something stupid.

For most of my life, after I'd figured out how to work with it, my ADD was my best friend. An ally. When I properly channeled it, it helped propel me to the NFL. But it could also be an enemy.

There is an old Zen saying: let go or be dragged. I had decided to let myself be dragged. Deep down, I had known this moment would come, but there was no way to be ready for it.

I had an addiction. I knew what I was saying to myself now was self-destructive to my well-being. But I felt powerless to end it. My mind was polluted by my desire to have things the way they should be.

I called the Albany Firebirds, the closest team to Pittsburgh.

The coach was excited; it turned out they didn't even have one kicker on the roster, and they were conducting tryouts the next day.

Karen and I drove two hours up to Erie, left Sadie in the comfort of grandma's care, and drove five hours to Albany. Déjà vu: I'd driven this part of the New York State Thruway when I was delivering vending machine junk food as a student at Gannon.

"How are you feeling?" Karen asked.

"I know how this will go," I said. "They're going to want to sign me. For 30 minutes, I'll blow them away. But I know my leg can't last a whole season. I'm delaying the inevitable."

Karen looked at me with a look she hadn't had on her face before. I could see the pain and anguish. "I don't want you to hurt your body anymore," she said.

Just a few nights earlier, I had woken up immobile. Back spasms made any movement torture. She rolled me off the bed and I lay in excruciating pain, motionless on the floor for about an hour. I had given up golfing, jogging, and other activities that hurt my back. Even holding Sadie hurt my back.

"We could use the money," I said.

Karen shook her head.

For the first time, Karen was telling me to stop. She wasn't the first to try to communicate with me. My body had been signaling me for months with shooting pains in my back and hips. Instead of feeling passionate about playing, I was obsessed and destructive. My success-at-all-costs mind-set was hurting myself and it was hurting others.

At the arena that evening, I outkicked another kicker. After the tryout, the coach walked Karen and me into his office. I was shocked to find myself unsure what I wanted him to say. Offer me a contract. No, wait. Don't; I need someone to tell me again that it's over.

I needed to get a consistent job that could take care of my family. This wasn't it.

"We want to sign you to a contract," the coach said as he leaned forward.

"Thanks, Coach. Sounds great. But, I have to ask. What if, say, the Raiders or the Cowboys or any other NFL team calls?" I said as I scratched my face.

"No problem," he answered. "We would grant you a release, and you could go back to the NFL."

For every question I had, he had an answer. "Let me talk this over with Karen out in the hall. I'll come back in five minutes and give you my decision."

Karen and I found a quiet spot behind the stadium bleachers to talk.

"I'll support you in whatever you decide to do," Karen said. "You've always told me it's the NFL or bust. This isn't the NFL. You played in the NFL. You've done it."

"But I'm quitting," I said.

"What else do you have to prove? It's hard watching you go through this pain."

I looked out at the indoor arena. The lights were off. I could barely see the goalposts. Is this the end? My heart felt nothing. Empty. I looked back at Karen. I placed my hands on her shoulders.

"You're right," I said. "It's time. But if I go back into his office and tell him no, he's going to talk me into signing a contract. I can't say no to playing football."

"Let's just leave!" Karen suggested.

"Without telling the coach?"

It went against everything I believed in communicating with coaches.

"You're right. I'll call him tomorrow and explain. Let's go."

I grabbed Karen's hand, and we went to the first exit door we could find in the arena. Locked.

The sound of our feet echoed as we raced down the dark, metal corridor passing closed up concession stands. I couldn't wait to get outside and see the sunlight. I vowed to no longer listen to that obsessive inner voice.

"Let's try that one."

Locked—and for good measure chained, too. We laughed. After we had run around the arena for 10 minutes, we found a custodian who directed us to an unlocked door. It was near the first door we'd tried, but we hadn't seen it. Above it was a large, illuminated "EXIT HERE" sign.

On the drive home to Pittsburgh, I stared out in silence at the road in front of me.

Karen left me alone in my head for the first dozen miles. Snow covered the grass along the side of the highway and the trees were bare. When I tried to think of what would be next, my mind was a void. Who was I without football?

Karen tried to lift me up. "You have more to offer the world than football."

I appreciated her confidence—and her example. Karen was the master of being open to new experiences.

I had faced change, fear, and heartbreak before. Each time, I'd been able to overcome it. But this feeling was different. I'd decided that I'd never play football again.

I'd been unwilling to recognize the physical limitations of my body. It was time I did. When we returned home, I thought back to the moment when we couldn't find the exit door. And then I thought, maybe I'm not locked in at all. Maybe an open door was always there, and all I had to do was gather the courage to move on.

CHAPTER 15
PILE ON

Being a football player made life seem so simple. You won or you lost. You made the team or you didn't. It was black and white. The rest of my world now seemed so complex by comparison.

In the month since I'd decided to quit football, I'd lived in the world known as *if only*. *If only* I had done this instead of that. I also spent countless hours thinking about the future and what I was going to do to replace my so-called football dream. I was stuck. *Move on. Let go,* I said to myself each day while driving, looking in the mirror, and eating. But I couldn't come up with anything that excited me. The "if onlys/what ifs" were too strong. A part of me was still hanging on to the past and dwelling on my NFL failures. The only break came when I was able to spend time with Karen and Sadie.

Over time, my obsession with *what could have been* lessened. I was slowly letting go. In my heart, I started to feel that time would heal my wounds and the shame of failure. Look at what I already had. I was married to the girl of my dreams. I had a beautiful daughter who was everything to me. I felt myself being propelled forward, and I was even excited about the possibilities.

It had only been a few weeks since I'd decided to hang up my cleats when the phone rang. It was my parents.

"We have something we need to tell you," my mom stated.

"I have cancer," my dad said.

No. That made no sense. He was healthy. He ran, he played in a softball league. At 55, he was one of the fittest guys his age I knew. He was in the military and he jumped out of planes. He was an action hero to me. He never called in sick for work. He never talked or complained of his problems.

"What kind?" I asked.

"Colon," my mom responded. "They're going to do a surgery next week and the hope is that it has not spread beyond the colon."

"We'll fight this," my dad said with his usual unwavering optimism before they hung up.

After I said goodbye, I told Karen the news.

The diagnosis was a wake-up call. I was done living in the past, in the life I never lived. I needed to live in the present moment. My world expanded again, just as it had when Sadie was born. I was reminded that life can be short and that it's about loving people. I wasn't just a football player. I was a son. A father. A husband. My identity expanded without an NFL job.

• • •

My father had the surgery at Allegheny General Hospital on Pittsburgh's North Side, just a few blocks away from Father Larry's childhood home and Amos's apartment when he lived in Pittsburgh. During the surgery, I sat in the private waiting room with my family. The doctor entered wearing his blue scrubs and a stoic look on his face.

"We removed part of your father's colon and the polyps," the doctor said. "Unfortunately, the cancer has spread to some lymph nodes and to his liver."

"What does that mean?" I asked.

"I'm afraid that once the cancer goes beyond the colon, it is terminal," he said.

I looked at the floor and then at my mom. She sat motionless.

"What do you mean by terminal?" I asked.

"Two years at the most," he replied.

He left the room. There had to be something we could do. There had to be a doctor somewhere or a treatment available that would cure my dad.

We embraced and wept.

I didn't sleep that night. I stared at the ceiling. My father was my best friend. I thought of the recent time when I was three weeks into training camp in Indianapolis. One evening, he called me and I told him how I was struggling and worried that the Colts might cut me. The next day, he traded shifts with a coworker and made a surprise seven-hour road trip from Erie to boost my spirits.

Once when he visited me at Pitt, I took him to a building called Forbes Quad, where a clear glass plate in the floor of a hallway overlooks the original home plate of Forbes Field, the home of the Pittsburgh Pirates from 1909 to 1970. He told me about how he had almost signed with the Pirates when he was just out of high school.

"I could have played in that game," he said. "When I finished high school, the Pirates drafted me and invited me to play for one of their minor-league teams. I told them no thanks. I joined the Army instead."

I knew he had been offered a contract, but I'd never asked him why he had turned it down. He told me, "It [the Army] paid more. I was the baby of five. My dad died when I was 12, so we needed the money."

As I thought about these moments, my mind went into denial mode. I refused to believe he would pass away soon.

With my dad given just two years to live, my focus shifted to seeing him as much as possible. And I wanted him to see Sadie as much as possible. She was his best medicine. Over the following months and years, we frequently took trips to Erie, and my parents visited often. My dad called me even more often, and he became super close with Sadie.

He tried every experimental drug that he qualified for, and though none of them cured his cancer, that didn't keep him from trying. I drove him back and forth to the Roswell Park Cancer Institute in Buffalo, where he was on the latest new drug. He even tried shark pills, which the manufacturer claimed could cure cancer. He drove to Montreal with my mom to visit St. Joseph's Oratory, where people claimed to have been cured. Rows of abandoned crutches and walking sticks in a chapel attested to their claims.

My dad, who'd had few hobbies outside of running and following sports, developed a fixation on rock gardens, roses, and the Virgin Mary. Two years into his diagnosis, he started a flower garden complete with roses and a statue of Mary.

It was totally out of the norm for him; for years, he'd put a lot of energy into making sure he would be home in time to watch a certain baseball game. But now, he was making sure he had the right rocks to decorate his garden and that his roses were taken care of.

• • •

"What do you think about another wedding, a real one with bagpipes?" I said as we sat on the deck with a couple of Honey Brown Ales.

"You mean with Scottish dancing?" Karen said.

"Let's have it in Erie. It would mean so much to my dad. We could have a big party and Father Larry could do the ceremony. To celebrate all of the people we are so lucky to have in our life. I just love you so much," I said. "You stuck with me through my football quest, and I know I have been selfish. I feel so lucky to spend the rest of my life with you."

Karen sat and just looked at me, smiling. "If you're asking me to marry you again, the answer is yes!"

• • •

The morning of our wedding day, August 9, 1997, Karen called me at my parents' house. She was getting ready at her mom's house across town.

"I just put on my wedding dress, you need to come see me."

"Is something wrong? I thought it was bad luck for the groom to see the bride in her dress before the wedding."

"Just come over."

Ten minutes later, I was in her mom's living room. Karen looked incredible in a white lace dress cut three inches above her knees.

"Notice anything?"

"You look gorgeous."

"Look closer!"

"Okay."

"Look how big my boobs are!"

"Is it the dress doing that? They look amazing. But do you think that's appropriate for the wedding?"

"It's not the dress. I'm pregnant!"

I hugged Karen.

"I'm excited too, it's just embarrassing," Karen cried.

"Don't worry, no one will ever know that you were pregnant for both of your weddings."

Later in the afternoon, Father Larry did the mass at St. Luke's Church in Erie. My father was my best man and Sadie, who was three, made the ideal flower girl, sporting a cherry lollipop in her mouth and a white sundress. We said, "I do," and a few moments later, the bagpiper burst out with a joyous "Scotland the Brave" as we walked down the aisle.

And then off we went to the reception. Destination: Karen's mom's backyard. She'd hung a wooden swing decorated with flowers on an enormous hundred-year-old cherry tree. The dance floor was an oversized piece of plywood placed on the grass. The DJ was anyone who walked near the boom box. It was perfect.

My dad stood up in his tuxedo and people started dinging their glasses. My mom sat in her seat and looked up at him while she fanned herself.

"Before I give a toast, I just want to remind Sean of his IOU."

He pulled a folded piece of paper out of his pocket. When he unfolded it, it reached all the way to the ground. Everyone laughed.

"These are things that I loaned Sean money for after he said, 'I'll pay you back. I promise.' A down payment on a Honda Civic. A second down payment on a different Honda Civic. The extra 18 credits of college tuition."

He pulled out a second piece of paper and unfolded it and it also went to the ground. Everyone laughed again. He folded them up and stuck them in his pocket.

He finished by reading an Irish blessing.

The bagpiper started playing again, so I began chanting, "Scottish dance! Scottish dance!"

Everyone called Karen's name. She whipped off her shoes and stepped onto the plywood stage. The bagpiper played the opening notes of a fast-paced, high-energy tune. Karen put her fists in the air and pointed her toes on her right foot as the bagpiper tuned.

I had a flashback to when she did it on stage in high school. As everyone clapped and went into a frenzy, I thought, *I love this girl.*

• • •

I prayed that my dad would be around in nine months to see his new grandchild.

With a second baby on the way, it was high time I got a better job to provide for my growing family. I was 27 years old, and my resume since graduating from college included: ice cream truck driver, UPS driver, restaurant deliveryman, college credit card hawker, auto parts delivery guy, painter, and bellman. My confidence that I could land a professional job using my degree was low.

With my cellphone sales experience, I tried to get a better sales job. I put my ADD to good use; I sent out over a hundred resumes and went on dozens of interviews. But they always asked, "What have you been doing the last five years?"

On March 26, 1998, while I was still waiting to hear back from the companies I had interviewed with, Karen went into labor at West Penn Hospital. We'd woken up to the weatherman telling us it would be 75 and sunny. Not a cloud in the sky. If the baby was a girl, she'd be called Summer.

We were all in the delivery room together: Karen, my mom, my dad, and me. Karen's parents were on their way. Karen pushed and breathed and pushed and breathed. The baby wouldn't come out.

"Go get another doctor!" the doctor yelled at one of the nurses.

There was a flurry of activity. We didn't know what was happening, and we were too scared to ask. With more doctors helping, forceps in hand, they managed to pull the baby out. She was blue, not breathing and not moving. Suddenly, she let out a cry.

Summer was here.

An hour after Summer was born, I was holding her in my arms when a pharmaceutical company called to offer me a sales job. After six years of unsteady employment, I felt lucky to have a steady job that could support my family at last. My father was two years into his battle with cancer, yet he was there to see Summer born, which we thought was a miracle. He stayed alive to meet her. The day of Summer's birth, I knew again how lucky my life was.

I stood next to him looking at Summer through the viewing window. "She's beautiful," he said as he choked up. "Karen and your girls, they are all so beautiful."

We continued staring through the glass.

"Being a dad is the best role you will play in your life."

One weekend in June 1999, when Summer was one, my parents came down to see the tiny house that we had just bought. My outlook on life was recovering while my father's health was weakening. My father looked frail and had lost weight. The lines of his skull were visible. His clothes looked baggy on him. It was the first time he looked sick. He no longer looked like a baseball slugger. My invincible all-star athlete dad.

But he still had his will. "Let's put up that light fixture," he said as he looked at the box on the floor. I'd bought a funky ceiling light from IKEA, which came with 20 pages of indecipherable directions, and he asked to help me install it. After five minutes, however, he sat down, exhausted. The cancer was starting to get the best of him physically, but it couldn't get the best of his attitude.

Over the next couple of months, he got weaker and weaker. But each time I saw him, I refused to believe what was happening. He kept telling me, "I'm going to beat this." I believed him. He was my hero. There was no way he would die. I engrossed myself in my new job and was busy with Karen, Sadie, and baby Summer.

My mom called on a Wednesday in August.

"Sean. Dad asked if you could bring the girls up today." My heart fell into my stomach. For the first time, the reality that my dad was dying hit me.

We packed the car and rolled into Erie two hours later. As we drove down my childhood street, Stafford Avenue, a man who looked like a much older and weaker version of my father walked toward the street waving at us.

I went upstairs, collapsed on my parents' bed, and started sobbing uncontrollably. My mom came up and sat next to me. She wrapped her arms around me and we cried.

My mom was going to be alone at just 56. I remembered how my parents used to talk about how much they looked forward to traveling together when they retired. Visiting their kids. Their grandkids. Going to Ireland. Getting older together. Her dream was shattered. I hugged her as I imagined her living alone in the house.

A few days later, my father lay in a hospital-style bed. Hospice was around now.

Cancer had taken over the room. An IV next to him. A rosary and a Bible on the nightstand. The always-on television, which usually showed a baseball or football game, was dark.

As I stood next to his bed, he asked me, "Are the girls here?"

"They're downstairs," I said.

"I want to go see them."

"Stay in bed," I told him. "We'll bring them up."

We were hesitant at first for the kids to see him; he wasn't looking or acting like himself, as he was on morphine. But we knew how badly he wanted to see the girls. Sadie, who was five, showed him the white paper plates she had decorated with brightly colored construction paper and glitter glue. He sat on the bed with them as long as he could until he needed to lie down again.

On the hot afternoon of August 10, 1999, three days after my brother's birthday, and just a few more days after the anniversary of our Erie wedding, my dad lay surrounded by his family. We linked our arms as we circled his bed: my mom, my brother and sister, Karen, some cousins, and his sisters. Tears streamed down my face as I squeezed my arms around my family. As the priest led us in prayer, we watched my dad take his last breath.

After the priest left and my family members made their way downstairs, my mom told me, "I asked him to give me a sign that he's okay."

A few hours later, the director of the funeral home arrived. We were standing on the porch—my mom, my brother and sister, Karen, and me. At the moment when they pulled away in the hearse, my mom said, "I smell roses."

One by one, we each smelled the scent as if petals had been placed in front of our faces. I have no doubt that this was the sign from my father that my mother had asked for.

At the funeral, I gave the eulogy along with my brother.

My father's life was over. I felt as if a part of me was gone. But I had to live on. Be gentle like him. Be kind. Instead of living two years as the doctor predicted, he'd lived for four. And lived he had. He'd lived with a positive attitude and I believed that was what had given him the extra time. To make sure his life went on, I resolved to live my life the same way by his example.

CHAPTER 16
NEW SEASON

We settled into our first house, a small two-bedroom house 15 minutes outside of Pittsburgh. The neighborhood was built in the 1940s and had rolling hills dotted with a mix of small brick colonial and Cape Cod–style homes with old pine trees in the yards. Our house had a wraparound paved driveway that we used for basketball, and we built a wooden swing set in the backyard. Our backyard sat on the only flat part of the neighborhood— so flat that it had been used as a landing strip for small planes during World War II. A lack of slope was a rarity in Pittsburgh. The house needed a lot of work on the inside: a new kitchen, new flooring, and new bathrooms. I did my best to renovate it, using what my father had taught me.

Just over a month had gone by since my father had passed away. I spent almost every moment thinking about him and how much I missed him. I knew that he wanted me to be the best dad I could be. He would want me to move on with my life.

My mom, who was still heartbroken, suffered another setback when her dad, my grandfather, died. He was 95. At 92, legally blind, he'd still been riding his bike around town to the German bakery and to nearby parks to pick elderberries for the pies that my grandma baked. And just a handful of weeks later, my sweet grandmother, who used to spend lazy summer days watching Chicago Cubs games on TV with me, passed away too. My sadness for my mom, combined with my own grief, paralyzed my mind. I spent most days in a fog.

I stuffed my emotions away. Almost every night, I experienced nightmares about the moment my father died.

Meanwhile, the last five years had been a whirlwind for Karen. She was on and off the yoga bandwagon. It had worked wonders for her when she'd first done it, when she was alone in Erie, but as life became busier and more hectic, it was hard to stay consistent.

Fall arrived. Every morning with the leaves turning yellow, the sun peeking through the white shades of our second-floor bedroom, I awoke to the sound of Karen downstairs breathing and moving. The first time I came down, she was drenched in sweat.

She told me she was doing power yoga with some guy named Baron Baptiste.

With a smile, she would ask me if I wanted to join in.

I walked past the action, opened the front door, grabbed the newspaper, made myself some coffee, and sat on the back patio. I went straight to the sports section of the *Pittsburgh Post-Gazette*.

She would go on and on about yoga. How it made her feel. One morning, she told me, "I want to teach yoga."

I signed myself up to be her biggest supporter. I could see the wheels of ambition turning just like my football career. She was going somewhere and I would be behind her for her journey.

Karen just didn't know where to train. It was 1999. Options were limited as there were no yoga studios in Pittsburgh at the time. She couldn't afford to go to India, so there had to be something else out there waiting for her.

That night after putting the kids to bed, I was watching *Monday Night Football* with a box of Snyder's Sourdough Pretzels and a can of beer. Karen talked to herself as she flipped through the pages of *Kripalu Center for Yoga* magazine.

"I'm going back up to Kripalu!" she exclaimed.

There was a weekend event coming up with a number of teachers at Kripalu in Massachusetts, where she'd gone with her mom a few years before. She signed up for the one called Power Yoga, taught by the guy whose practice she did each morning, Baron Baptiste.

"You should go," I said. "I'll hold down the fort at home."

A few weeks later, she made the eight-hour drive to the mountainous Berkshires area of western Massachusetts, dotted with quaint villages.

When she returned, she talked my ear off about her weekend.

"I loved it. Baron Baptiste said he just started leading teacher trainings. So I'm signing up for his first one."

"And you may be interested in this."

Pause.

"I told him about your messed-up back from football, and he said he taught yoga to the Philadelphia Eagles."

"Really?"

Although it was just a weekend, Karen came home with enough confidence to get her feet wet and start teaching the basics: downward dog, upward dog, triangle pose, etc.

She stapled posters on telephone poles around the neighborhood.

Yoga with Karen Conley at the Blackridge Community Center
Wednesdays 6 p.m.
Suggested donation $5

I was impressed with her energy. She was working on a dream. Determined.

She would arrive at 5:30 p.m. and stack the metal chairs, put the tables away, and sweep the dusty tile floor. Most of her students had never done a downward dog before. Some were overweight. Some had not exercised in years. Yet, within a few months, her classes were packed.

People wanted yoga more than once a week, so Karen started teaching at our gym two days a week. We'd go to the gym together and drop off the kids in the gym's day care. Karen would teach yoga while I lifted weights. After my hour of tossing around dumbbells and barbells, puffing out my chest, and glancing at my biceps in the mirror, I would come down at the end of Karen's class and wait outside. Ladies would file out of class with giant smiles on their faces. Each week, more and more ladies walked out—first two or three, soon 20 or more.

I wondered, maybe this yoga works. After the last woman left, I went in and helped Karen reorganize the room.

"When are you going to take class?" Karen asked.

"Soon," I replied.

"Soon? Sounds like we're making progress. You used to say 'never'; 'never' turned to 'someday,' and now we've made it all the way to 'soon,'" Karen responded.

Karen continued pressing me to take up yoga in the following months, but I had a new obsession. I was engrossed with my job in pharmaceutical sales. It helped me keep my mind off my father's death and my lost NFL career. But I was just stuffing the emotion away. And to a much lesser degree, working in sales turned out to be a way to feed my competitive spirit. There were ongoing contests to see who could convince, persuade, or entice doctors to prescribe the most medicine in their territories, and for a time, I threw myself into these practices without questioning the ethics of them. After leaving the NFL rat race, I was now focused on making as much money as possible. Within just a couple of years, I was a top salesman. I was able to pay off our student loans, get our first mortgage, and begin a 401K. My company was generous and good to me, but I got suckered into the race for more. As a football player, I'd believed that achieving goals was the only way to be happy, and working as a salesman brought the quest for goals back to the surface. I chased dollars, hoping for a bigger bonus or to win the next sales contest. I was good at it. But it didn't bring me any more happiness.

I started to feel uneasy about the methods of selling. My job was to schmooze doctors, taking them out to fancy dinners, buying the most expensive bottles of wine, bringing $500 lunches for their entire staff—all to persuade them to like me and therefore prescribe my company's drug. I won a sales contest that awarded me an all-expenses-paid vacation with Karen to St. Thomas in the Virgin Islands. There we found we could go on any excursion we wanted and eat in any restaurant. We hired our own private captain for the day to take us snorkeling and to visit the Soggy Dollar Bar on the beach of Jost Van Dyke, where we drank painkillers all day and played ring toss among the white sand and crystal-blue water with bobbing yachts anchored offshore. At the glitzy resort hotel we stayed in, we could order *anything* we wanted to our rooms. In the hotel lobby, a couple of my fellow sales reps asked me, "Have you ordered a bottle of Dom Perignon to your room yet?"

"What's that?"

Turned out it was a $200 bottle of champagne. It didn't sit right with me that we charged such high rates for our medicine when people had issues with their health. I knew what my company charged and I saw the bills my parents had to pay just to try to keep my dad alive. People were dying, and there we were soaking up rays and drinking expensive champagne and rum. But I tagged along, enjoying myself too much to question what I was doing. I used my taste for competition and winning to keep moving forward toward what I perceived as success.

After the trip, I went back and met with physicians who complained about how expensive our drug was. And with a straight face, I replied as I was trained to reply: The high costs were due to the costs of research and development. But I knew how we blew money. I made more money than most of the doctors I met and certainly more than the nurses. It was upside down. We had sales meetings in cities like Las Vegas and San Diego in lavish hotels with open bars and private concerts by bands like the Eagles and Huey Lewis and the News.

At the time, the biotech drug industry was emerging. These companies were using genetic engineering to create new therapies that could treat diseases such as HIV and cancer. I wanted in the game. Many ambitious sales representatives considered biotech sales jobs the Holy Grail. They paid more, gave stock options, and they were always getting glamorous press coverage on CNBC Business. The opportunity to sell drugs that could help cancer patients like my dad only made me want one of these jobs even more. I worked 50-hour weeks to win contests. When I wasn't at work, I thought about work. It worked. My sales numbers bolstered my resume, and by the fall of 2000, after just a little over two years at the big pharmaceutical company, I scored a job with a hot biotech start-up that was considered a Wall Street darling. I thought I had made it.

One afternoon while I was driving to a sales call in Canton, Ohio, the home of the NFL Hall of Fame, as I reached for the radio dial, I felt a sharp pain like someone was stabbing my low back with a knife. I had been experiencing spasms multiple times a month, but this one was a Hall of Famer for pain. My lower body locked up like Fort Knox. I pulled into a rest area and gasped for air until the pain stopped.

I'd found that the only way to get relief beyond the sleepy pills was to lie down and wait for the spasms to subside. Just a couple of weeks earlier, I'd had to sit on the grass during a Seal concert while Karen danced and sang. Standing on my feet for long periods had become dreadful. I feared going anywhere I couldn't sit down. *I'm only in my 30s*, I thought, *and I can't stand.*

Karen continued to enthusiastically push yoga on me. And I couldn't get the thought out of my mind of the Philadelphia Eagles doing yoga. Maybe it would help?

"Okay," I finally told her after I got home that day. "I'll go to your class on Monday."

● ● ●

I slid into the room at the last moment, trying not to be noticed. But the 20-some ladies watched me as I awkwardly set up my mat in the back right-hand corner of the room. I hoped that they wouldn't stare at me once class began. I considered whether I still had time to bolt before it would be obvious.

The woman next to me asked me if it was my first time. Was it that obvious?

She assured me that I would be okay. She looked organized like everyone else. Towel, water bottle, smiling, relaxed.

"Good morning, everyone! How's everyone doing?" Trademark smile from Karen.

I had my socks on. Everyone else was in bare feet. *Shit.* I wasn't much of a barefoot person, but I reluctantly took them off.

"Child's pose."

It was *on*. No turning back now.

"Set your knees wide apart. Place your forehead on your mat. Allow your hips to sink down toward your heels."

I got myself into position and felt a strong pull down my hamstrings. If this was supposed to feel *restful*, I definitely wasn't going to make it. What had I gotten myself into?

My hips stuck up toward the white dropped ceiling and fluorescent lights. I glanced over at the mirror on my right. I looked like a broken-down Volkswagen Bug. Meanwhile, the stretch felt intense in my lower back but at the same time strangely good and therapeutic. I held my breath, thinking it would get me through the pose. But holding my breath had the opposite effect.

"Come into downward-facing dog," Karen said.

"Place your hands flat and spread out your fingers," Karen instructed.

"Set your feet hip-width distance apart, and press your tailbone up to the sky."

I glanced at the mirror.

My back was rounded. Not because I didn't know how to do the pose—I had done it before a few times with Karen years ago—I was just so tight. My shoulders began to scream. My neck stiffened.

"If you have tight hamstrings, bend your knees," Karen said.

If?

She walked around the room and helped each student one by one making quick adjustments. Then she led us through a short and fast-moving warmup series called Vinyasa Bs. They were quick, one movement per breath.

"Upward-facing dog."

Ouch.

"Press back to downward-facing dog. Step your right leg forward. Come into warrior one."

Yikes. My arms were shaking. Was it just me that felt like this was a torture session instead of a yoga class? I glanced around, and all the women looked so calm. I had been a pro athlete and these ladies were putting me to shame.

She instructed us into a pose called crescent lunge.

I looked around. People willingly do this? Why?

"Step your right foot forward. Reach your arms to the sky."

I wasn't going to make it. Sweat rolled down my forehead. I held my breath. *I'm never doing this again.* The ladies around me made it look so easy. They seemed to float and glide. Karen said, "Just grab your foot." *That* foot?

My mobility was even more limited than I'd known. *If this was how I felt at 30,* I thought, *what was I in for at 40 or 50?* I couldn't be doing this right. *Don't we get any breaks?*

I slugged my way through the next half hour.

At one point in class, I fell over trying too hard, and knocked over my water bottle in the process, which was as loud as a bowling pin. There were times I wanted to crawl out of the classroom.

I was beginning to discover that it was mental just as much as physical. "Final relaxation," Karen said.

For the first couple of minutes, I looked around to see what everyone else was doing, moved my yoga block, wiped the sweat from my face, and fidgeted some more. Then I stared at the ceiling thinking about what I had to do next. I finally closed my eyes. After a moment or two, I let out an exhale. My breath slowed. My muscles slacked. I had a brief moment without any desire to be anywhere else. I didn't feel like I had somewhere to get to. I didn't feel stuck in the past. I wasn't wishing for a specific future. It was a feeling of being immersed in the moment like when I was looking into Karen's eyes, holding one of my kids, watching a sunset, or kicking a football when I was 10.

I couldn't put it into words, but I felt euphoric. I really liked this feeling. I *might* even give this another shot.

After class, I waited for everyone to leave and then I hobbled out of the room feeling one part defeated, one part rewarded.

The next morning, I would wake up with healthy soreness in muscles I didn't know I had.

At home and in the car Karen talked nonstop about yoga.

In the next few weeks, she started talking about opening her own studio. But she would talk herself out if it because she felt she didn't know enough yet, or Pittsburgh wasn't ready for a yoga studio, or it just wasn't the right time.

I felt a role reversal coming on.

I assured her she knew enough. "Let's just drive around the area and look at spaces."

We drove around for a couple of hours, and when we were about to call it a day, we saw a sign in a worn-down mini shopping plaza on a hill next to a gas station: "For Rent: Irv Weiner Real Estate." We peeked in the windows. The space was just big enough for 25 people to put down their mats.

"I'll do all the renovations. I'll put in a new floor, paint the walls."

I was determined to keep nudging Karen toward opening a studio. She had the "it" factor. Yoga got her juices flowing the way football did for me. This was her passion. She had discovered it through her own struggle of being a new, overwhelmed, and confused mother. I felt lucky to be able to give back in our relationship. I wasn't totally sold yet on yoga myself, but I was sold on supporting her dream.

We stared in the windows. Karen peered in, using her hands to block the glare from the sun. She said nothing for a minute. I could practically hear the gears turning as her hope and enthusiasm grew, imagining what she could make of the space.

"Let's do it!" Karen said.

I called Irv the next day and it turned out that the rent was cheap, as the place had been vacant for months. Irv was a tough negotiator at first, but I eventually managed to knock off a couple hundred dollars and we signed the lease.

A few weeks later, Karen came home from the grocery store carrying brown paper bags, one of which contained two bags of oranges, enough to feed a family of monkeys for weeks. She sat down at the table and started peeling and eating.

"Florida called and they're out of oranges," I said.

"Yeah, I don't know what it is but I'm craving them," she said.

For the next few days, Karen had a hankering for oranges and nectarines. She was eating them at every meal and snack.

"My body is telling me something. It wants vitamin C . . . and I'm a couple weeks late."

Her female intuitive powers had been right. She was pregnant with our third baby. Sadie was seven and Summer was three.

For months, we had gone back and forth on having another baby: should we, shouldn't we. We were still learning on the fly how to raise two kids. Could we handle three? We weren't exactly stable, but we just loved having kids so much, our excitement about expanding our family won out. During our back-and-forth, we adopted a yellow lab named Bailey from a farm 20 minutes west of Erie.

Karen was soon to be opening a new studio and pregnant at the same time. I had no doubt she could still make it happen, even though she continued to question herself at times. Her spinning and kickboxing classes were always packed because people loved her high-energy, enthusiastic, and positive instruction. She'd established a reputation as one of the best kickboxing and spinning instructors in the city. She was Wonder Woman.

I worked at the studio alone after my day job selling drugs. I alternated between listening to sports radio and—*gasp*—yoga music: Enya, Krishna Das, Bhagavan Das, and, as far as I knew at the time, maybe even Häagen-Dazs. I removed the old tile floor and replaced it with a wood floor. I painted the studio walls sky blue and constructed a reception area. I scrubbed the toilets, which looked like they hadn't seen a flush in a decade. After about two months of work, it was ready. Because of how the practice made people feel, we called it Amazing Yoga.

We had a grand opening party on Saturday, May 11, complete with balloons, streamers, Ritz crackers and saltines, and boxed wine. The only people who showed up were Karen's family who lived in the Pittsburgh suburbs and a handful of our friends and neighbors.

"Oh shit. We know everybody here. Are you sure we made the right decision?" Karen asked.

I put my arm around her. "You're sharing something you love. It will work out."

The next week, the studio opened. Eight classes spread out from Monday to Saturday.

On Monday, the day the studio was to open its doors for the first time, Karen had one class on the schedule: 9:30 a.m. During my meeting with physicians at the Cleveland Clinic, my mind drifted to Karen waiting for people to show up at her first class. I was pulling for her.

After my meeting, I walked back to my car in the parking garage and buckled up, ready to head to my next meeting. My watch said 9:33. If Karen didn't call, that meant someone had shown up. At 9:35, the phone rang. It was Karen. Not good.

"How are you?" I asked.

"Nobody's here but me!" she cried. "I knew this was a bad idea."

Her voice echoed. I pictured Karen sitting on the wood floor surrounded by the blue walls, alone. Karen had encouraged my dream for years, and now I was the life coach.

"It can only go up from here. It will make for a beautiful story that your first class had zero students. Today, you just planted your first seed. My first field goal attempt was a disaster, but it was just a small beginning."

Karen sniffled on the other end of the phone.

"People will be attracted to your studio because of your selfless love of yoga," I told her. And when she didn't seem convinced, I went on, "You have so much genuine passion and love for yoga that it's infectious."

I could hear Karen breathing. After a pause, I added, "You even convinced me to do it. That's a miracle."

CHAPTER 17
TRADE

sat up straight in bed with a jolt. I was sweating and felt disoriented. My heart was racing. It was three or four o'clock in the morning.

It was the same night terror that I had experienced for months now. I stood over my father on his deathbed. He was lying on his back, his body and face yellow and jaundiced, looking nothing like I remembered him. I would see him again take his last breath, and at that moment, I'd wake up, letting out a scream and sob that woke Karen and the kids.

The next morning, Karen suggested, "Why don't you come to class tonight?"

The studio was a couple months old. I was sticking to my janitorial, maintenance duties, and hadn't practiced yet at the new studio. It had slipped on my priority list. I agreed.

That evening while the babysitter watched the girls, I found myself in the back right corner of the studio. The room was packed, as I knew it would be. Karen's dream was in motion.

"Come into warrior three pose," Karen said.

In warrior three, you attempt to stand on one leg and reach your arms straight out in front of you while your leg (the one that's off the floor) extends straight back. If all goes according to plan, you look like a human letter T.

"For the modification, if you have back issues, you can bring your hands to prayer position instead of extending your arms out," Karen said.

This was yoga; it was supposed to be good for me. I didn't want to do the less challenging option. Modification, shmodification. I didn't want to *modify*, I wanted to *intensify*.

I extended my arms out like all the women in the room who made the movement look so effortless, as if they were ballerinas on the stage of the Royal Opera House.

My lower back tied into a knot and it felt like all the blood in my body was racing to my lumbar. I stayed in the pose. The pain grew.

"Five more breaths," Karen said.

My face contorted and I looked like I was having a bowel movement as I held my breath. Beads of sweat rolled down my face. My leg shook like Jell-O.

I continued class with my inflamed back. I did every pose. As class went along, for each pose, I had an expectation or an image in my head of how I wanted to look in that pose, so I would try to go deeper. I felt pain in the pose but kept going, because I had been taught to believe in no pain, no gain.

After I pushed, forced, struggled, and muscled my way through the class, Karen finally instructed us to come down to the floor.

"Pigeon pose."

We entered the pose from downward dog.

"Put your right knee on the floor next to your right wrist."

After more instruction, I was on the floor with my right knee bent and my left leg straight. My chest was close to the floor and my head was on the floor. The sensation in my right hip was intense. The physical awareness sparked emotions. It was as if the pose hit the play button on a tape recorder of my life. I first began to relive the class and the frustration I experienced at thinking I couldn't do all the poses. Then I felt anger about my dad being gone too soon. I cursed myself, for the millionth time, for my decision to over-train in my pursuit of NFL glory.

"Ten breaths," Karen said.

Breathe. I'd heard Karen suggest this many times before. It had always sounded like a waste of time. But if I was going to be here for 10 breaths, I might as well give this breathing thing a shot. I relaxed in my own pool of sweat.

We did a couple of other poses that assisted in cooling down.

And then Karen brought us to final relaxation.

For a brief moment, my mind raced, reverting to old thought patterns. But my body was fatigued from all the poses and movements and soon my mind started to rest too.

In the following weeks, I practiced two times a week. I began to understand the effectiveness of breathing. I learned to go only as far into the pose as I comfortably could, until my body signaled me to stop. Over the coming months, after class, instead of feeling wounded and beat up as I did after lifting weights, I felt strong, light, and rejuvenated. My muscle spasms and back pain, which had been happening two or three times a day, were down to just once a day, then once a week. Then months later, gone. I fulfilled my need for a strong physical workout with yoga; it was a challenging practice, but I wasn't destroying my body in the process. I dropped my gym membership.

I also experienced a different, unexpected kind of healing.

I didn't realize it in the moment, but on my yoga mat, over time, the more I practiced, the more I would be able to grow my awareness. Before, I might not have noticed that my mind was drifting. But, it wasn't just a class or a pose. I could work on being present wherever I was. This awareness was the key to it all.

I realized that I didn't need to wait for significant events to happen in order to change. When my dad was diagnosed with cancer, I appreciated him more. But I didn't have to wait for tragedy to strike in order to do that. When our kids were born, I'd learned about being present in the moment. But I didn't have to wait for a miracle like that, either. *No more waiting* became my new mantra. I also didn't have to wait to be happy. Instead of focusing on thoughts like *I'll be happy once we have our first house*, or *I'll be happy when I make an NFL roster*, I discovered I could be happy at any moment I chose.

The despair I felt from losing my dad shifted to feelings of gratitude. One evening, I just sat on my bed and cried. I hadn't cried since the funeral. I just let it out. I began thinking of all that he'd taught me and all the great memories I had with him. My nightmares went away.

As 2002 drew to a close, Karen's doctor suggested that she be induced. The baby was looking large. Sadie had come out looking like she was ready to get her driver's license, and Summer had had wide shoulders, which had caused the obstruction. They thought the safest bet was to have this baby earlier.

Everyone thought Karen was having a boy. People would say, "The way you are carrying, it is definitely a boy." Some would rub Karen's belly and predict, "It's a boy." Wrong. On December 18, 2002, No-Name Conley was born. She was gorgeous. Weighing in at a little over seven pounds, she had red skin, no hair, and was precious.

We'd only had a boy's name picked out: Jack. We scrambled for ideas. At first, all we could agree on was that the name should begin with the letter S.

I asked Karen, "What about Scout?"

As in Scout from *To Kill a Mockingbird* by Harper Lee, one of our favorite books and favorite characters from high school English. Scout Finch was compassionate, curious, adventurous, courageous, and spunky. Scout it was.

● ● ●

One day in late spring of 2004, I was driving back toward Pittsburgh from my sales territory in the Laurel Mountains outside of town. Pittsburgh had transformed from bare trees and gray colors to an infinite variety of shades of green and flowers.

I pulled into the studio parking lot and was repairing a rusty metal bathroom stall, preparing it for a new paint job, when Karen called me on my cellphone.

"What are you doing?" she asked.

"Hanging out in the bathroom," I said.

"One of the teachers got a new job. I need a new teacher. Like now," she said. "You have to start teaching next week."

I laughed.

"I don't have any other options. I'll have to close the studio," she said. "And you'll be great."

"I like just practicing yoga, being the maintenance man, the janitor, and the business guy," I replied.

"Sorry, your training starts tonight. In the living room, once the kids are in bed."

That evening, after we tucked Sadie, Summer, and Scout into bed, Karen gave me the basics, showing me a sequence that I could teach along with some information about alignment and safety. I started teaching five days later.

On my drive to the studio, I rehearsed the class in my head over and over. Poses danced in my head: triangle, down dog, chair pose, etc. I'd written it all down in an old football notebook. I had a plan. If I got stuck, I'd just say, "Hey, everyone, downward dog." Then no one would see me cheating by looking in my notebook for the next pose.

How hard could this be? When I was a captain at Pitt, I had to speak in front of the team. In my current profession, I had done dozens of presentations in front of doctors and surgeons who had MDs, PhDs, DOs, etc., and I talked about pharmacokinetics, randomized double-blinded phase-three studies, pharmacodynamics response, and antiviral cytokines. Asking people wearing leotards and gym trunks to get into pigeon pose couldn't be that hard.

I arrived at the studio a half hour early.

Fifteen women showed up with their water bottles, mats, and towels. Ready. One of them asked with one hand on her hip before she entered the yoga room, "Where's Kathy?" And another, "Are *you* the teacher tonight?"

The ladies sat on their knees, whispering to one another before class began.

"Let's start in child's pose."

Things seemed to be going okay, I thought, until about 20 minutes into class, a woman blurted out, "You didn't teach the second side!"

I had forgotten three poses on the left side.

"I did that on purpose," I said. "It was just a test to see who was paying attention."

A few ladies laughed, and I exhaled.

Then I forgot the next pose.

"Come into downward dog."

I opened up my notebook. *Aha!* "Crescent lunge."

After the ladies were all in the pose, I said, "This pose is named after a famous French pastry."

Crickets.

"It's actually pronounced *croissant* lunge."

A few more laughs.

I'd always thought yoga was supposed to be serious. Whenever I peeked into Karen's yoga books lying on the coffee table, the yogis had serious looks like they were trying to solve a math equation while trying out for the Cirque du Soleil.

Screw it, I thought. Everyone likes to laugh. I'm telling another one.

I wrapped up class with a brief guided meditation.

Afterward, the lady who had questioned if I was teaching, a regular attendee named Judy, approached me and with a straight face said, "Your class was different . . . it was funny."

I wasn't sure if it was a compliment or not.

Afterward, I reviewed the class in my mind. I was upset about all my screw-ups. But I knew I could fix those.

I continued to sprinkle in a handful of jokes each class. Hearing people laugh gave me joy, not because they laughed at my jokes but because I liked the idea that maybe they got a little break from their concerns and worries. One smile was worth it. *Maybe I can teach.* Maybe my classes could be a place where one could laugh and smile a little bit.

The next couple of classes went a little better with the exception of when I stepped on a woman's glasses. And the one time I accidentally bumped into a woman who was trying to balance in tree pose.

• • •

Class was finished. I stood by the exit door thanking everyone as they left one by one. A tall, silver-haired lady, Linda, was still near her mat, seemingly in no hurry to leave. She had been coming to class every week for months, but rarely spoke a word to anyone. Once everyone was out of the yoga room, she approached me.

I noticed a tear running down her cheek.

"I just wanted to thank you for opening this studio. If it wasn't for yoga," she said, "I would not have been able to deal with the loss of my daughter."

I didn't know what to say.

I hugged her and she smiled.

From this point forward, I decided to teach each class with Linda in mind. That by chance, someone might be benefiting in a way I couldn't know.

I had a passionate déjà vu. It reminded me how I felt when I first discovered my gift for kicking footballs. I never thought I could love a job more than football, but teaching yoga was different. When I taught, it was about the people in the yoga room and not me trying to accomplish a goal.

As I continued to teach, at random times, sometimes after class, or at the grocery store, students would share with me why they did yoga. One guy was a stressed-out lawyer who told me that yoga was the only time of day when his mind relaxed and he didn't have to think about anything else. One woman shared with me that yoga helped her through a messy divorce. Another found yoga to help her handle the pain and anxiety of being laid off from her job.

It was clear to me. I had found a way to give back. I could help others with physical injuries and relief from their busy minds.

As I got deeper into yoga and meditation, I realized something was missing at my day-to-day job. My heart wasn't in sales. I began thinking about teaching yoga full-time. I shared this one evening with Karen, along with all my misgivings.

If I quit, I told her, we were going to make much less money.

We would have to buy our own insurance.

There'd be no more company car.

No more 401K and stock options.

And I was a guy. A male full-time yoga teacher?

Karen was worried about our insurance and our security. But she understood how I had disagreed with some of the practices in the industry and she was excited to go on another adventure with me. This time, together.

For the next sales meeting, our company invited Mike Eruzione, former captain of the 1980 US Olympic gold-medal-winning hockey team, as a guest speaker. Eruzione had an enthusiastic Boston accent, full cheeks, and dark, slicked-back hair. He had played in the famous Miracle on Ice, where a team of 20 ragtag, fresh-faced college kids, through heart and determination, found a way to beat the seasoned, professional, supposedly unbeatable Soviet hockey team in the winter wonderland of Lake Placid, New York. Two weeks prior to the Olympics, the Soviets had beat the United States 10–3, and a year earlier, the Soviets had crushed an NHL All-Star team 6–0. This team pulled off the impossible. It's still considered one of the greatest upsets in sports history.

At the sales meeting, Eruzione captivated me. I started taking notes as he spoke, because his words made an impact.

"Our coach, Herb Brooks, said, 'Great moments are born from great opportunities,'" Eruzione began. "We had heart and determination, but above all else, we believed in ourselves and each other. We believed we could accomplish something that no one in the world thought was possible. Individually, we can be good, but collectively, we can be champions. It wasn't a miracle. We weren't lucky. It was a process."

His words reminded me of my football days, and I could feel the old fire light up. Eruzione had transitioned from sports to professional jobs, and he said something that went straight to my core: "If you don't want to be here, if you don't want to buy into it, then leave. There are thousands of people who would like to be in your shoes. Because not only are you hurting your opportunity to succeed, you are also diminishing the opportunities of the people you work with. Surround yourself with people whose objectives are the same as yours. Whatever you do in life, put your whole heart into it. And if your heart is not in it, quit. Let someone else do it. Find something that feeds your passion."

I knew he was right.

Afterward, I scribbled down all of our family expenses on a piece of paper. Health insurance, car payment, utilities, food. Then I looked at the difference in revenue if I quit. It would be a huge cut. And then I thought about my game plan, all the hats I would need to wear: accountant, plumber, cleaner, maintenance man, teacher, and human resource manager. It was daunting, but even so, I decided that in exactly two months I would quit. I would make sure that my territory was all set nicely for the next person, and then I would resign.

Two months came and went, and the time arrived to resign. I opened my company email and saw a message titled "Hawaii."

"Congratulations, you've won a trip to a convention in Hawaii," it read.

I froze. I felt the golden handcuffs tighten around my wrists. If I were to go, I would be a phony. I sat with it and my mind bounced around like a basketball. I'd worked hard getting to this point in my career; I had a great salary, benefits, and future growth potential. Could I give it up to venture into the unknown?

For the past year or so, Karen and I had been hoping to have one more child. "Maybe I should wait to quit in a year or so, just in case we have another kid," I said.

In the morning, I went to yoga, hoping for clarity. I went home, walked into my home office, and closed the door. I stared out the window and looked at the trees I had planted in the spring—pines, willow, and a giant sequoia that I'd ordered from a tree farm in California. I admired their strength, as they stood tall in the wind. My stomach got queasy.

I called my boss and resigned. She was shocked, but my decision was final.

I had given up great security and had no idea what might lie before me as a yoga teacher. But I did believe what Mike Eruzione believed: If I followed my passion, it would all work out.

● ● ●

About two weeks later, on a crisp fall afternoon, we took the kids to the pumpkin patch. As we walked the fields looking for the family pumpkin, Karen said to me, "I think I may be pregnant."

When the time came for Karen's sonogram, we took our three girls to the hospital: Sadie, Summer, and Scout. On the way, we argued over what to name the baby; we were thinking of a girl's name that started with S. I threw out the idea of Samantha. "We could call her Sam," I said.

Once we were in the office, the nurse applied the mystery goo to Karen's baby bump. She asked us if we wanted to know the sex of the baby. The girls all yelled, "Yes!"

As the nurse conducted the scan, she gazed at all the girls in the room hovering over Karen. We heard her mutter under her breath, "Hmm, I can't believe this."

"Believe what?" I asked.

"Hold on, stay here, I'll be right back," she said.

"Where does she think we'll go?" I asked.

A tall doctor strutted in. He grabbed the transducer and did a quick once-over that lasted less than 10 seconds. We all looked at him expectantly.

"It's a boy," he said. So much for Samantha.

And then as quick as he came in, he left like a sly wizard.

● ● ●

This is who I am now, a former NFL kicker, father of four, and full-time yoga instructor. I look back on that little boy with ADD who tried to ditch his Ritalin pills at lunch, the teenager kicking footballs alone on an ice-covered field in Erie, the young man desperate to prove himself in the roaring arenas of the NFL, and the father and husband eager to support his family and win sales contests—and I am grateful that all these past selves are present in me. I'm grateful for all I've lived, suffered, and learned, but most of all, I am grateful for this moment: for the feeling of those I love around me. I am grateful for right now.

ACKNOWLEDGMENTS

This book would not have been possible without my soul mate, best friend, and awesome wife, Karen. Thank you for being the sounding board when I needed to vent about writing plateaus. I am grateful for your help filling in the gaps, fact checks, and sharing passages from your journal. I will cherish our early morning coffee talks consisting of memory extraction and "Hey remember when?" From reading early, middle, and late drafts, to help piece together stories, to loving and encouraging me.

A special thank you to my children: Sadie, Summer, Scout, and Jack for putting up with countless conversations about *dad's book*. And for the dozens of times "Which book cover to do you like best?" I hope this book will give you guidance to not make the same mistakes I did. I hope it makes you feel proud and gives you some laughs.

I would like to mention my father who I miss dearly. He taught me that life was about being kind and loving.

Thank you mom for loving me no matter what. Thank you for putting up with me and I hope I didn't cause you too much stress back in the day. My mom is suffering from late-stage Alzheimer's. She loved reading books and I am sad she won't be able to read this. My mom helped make this book possible from saving everything in her attic from yellowed newspaper clipping, my faded notebook from the Detroit Lions, media guides, dusty VHS tapes of games, and photos all stored in boxes. So many photos and memorabilia that helped confirm my memory of every game. I felt like Indiana Jones putting all the pieces together.

Thank you to my brother Ty and sister Amy for living with my restlessness and know that I am so thankful to have you both in my life.

None of this would have been possible without my some of my friends. Andy Tsouris, for being my only friend at first when I transferred to Pitt and all the laughs and support. Thanks to John Bruner for always being there from holding footballs, driving through the night for an NFL workout to being my sports shrink when I needed one. I am grateful for Father Larry Richards for always being the person I could turn to during those dark and desperate teenage years.

A very special thanks to my coach-mentor-friend Amos Jones. You are the owner of the world's biggest heart. You took a chance on a long-shot walk on kicker with new experience and you believed in me. You treated me as a son. I feel blessed and cherish our lifetime friendship.

I would like to thank all my teammates and coaches from my prized days in Erie to Gannon University to the University of Pittsburgh and on all the professional teams.

Thanks to everyone on the Lyons Press team who has worked so hard to bring *The Point After* into fruition. I'm especially grateful to Gene Brissie, for believing in the book, and always being available. Thank you to Alex Bordelon for your patience and precision.

I am indebted to three valuable editors who helped shape the book. Anne Horowitz, thank you for your kindness, generosity, and doing all the initial heavy lifting. Without Anne, this book would be filled with run on sentences and incoherent thoughts. Thanks to Alessandra Lusardi for pushing me to take the book to the next level. Becky Cole, much gratitude for helping carry the book across the goal line with your invaluable advice, edits, smarts, and intuition. Without each of them, I would still be staring blankly at my computer screen, "What do I do next? I also want to extend my thanks to Chris Peterson and Rachel Stout.

Thank you to my stellar agent, Jane Dystel for responding in mere seconds after I sent a query letter begging her to take on my book. Your belief in my story and me was invaluable. I am indebted to you and your entire team including Amy Bishop, and Miriam.

I have to thank the host of friends I have used as readers. And also apologize that you had to read it early on when it was clunky and painful. True friends. My thanks go to Melanie Taylor, Billy Jenkins, and Kim Kir. Thank you to the talented author Angela Small for not just reading but sharing invaluable advice to a rookie writer. To Lee Gutkind, aka the Godfather of creative nonfiction for the instrumental advice on how to tell stories and reminding me that I can't make anything up.

Thank you to all the people that have been to our yoga studios, retreats, and teacher trainings. Thank you for allowing me to share my love of yoga with you and I hope that you have found benefit in it. Much Gratitude.

This book would not exist without my friends Kelly Ramsey and Shawna Kenny. When the book was in the early stages and was more of an idea and scattered discombobulated words on paper, you were the magicians and mentors that put the story into motion with your honest tough-love feedback and vision. I am eternally grateful.

As I look over this list, I can't believe how many people have touched my life in so many ways. Thank you all!

INDEX